THE METHOD

By

Vilius Komskis

FOREWORD

At no other point in the history of mankind have we had to deal with so many systems specifically designed to distract, addict, and influence us. The most popular people in antiquity never had to open their devices and instantly compare themselves to thousands of people. Never have our minds been so cluttered and under stress as they are now. It is no wonder that our generation is more likely to suffer from anxiety, depression, and stress than those that came before. Fortunately, you can thrive despite these challenges; everything you need to succeed is already within you. It's only an unhealthy imbalance of time, emotions, effort, and finances that's holding you back.

For the past couple of years, I've been exploring numerous methods for self-improvement, ranging from habit-forming to new diets, in an effort to manage the overwhelming anxiety, stress, and bouts of depression that have been plaguing me. I didn't always have these problems; they have surfaced recently–coincidentally, around the time when social media and mobile devices became the norm. But while the digital world played its part, it wasn't the only cause. Life today has plenty of stressors. As we enter school, and even as we graduate, we place more and more expectations on ourselves. Whether you like it or not, the pattern of college - job - moving out - getting married - kids is viewed as the gold standard. And if at any point you fall behind the "perfect" timeline, you'll feel like you're failing in some way. Not only that, but on a day-to-day basis, you're comparing yourself to people on social media and reading stories about millionaires being born from some new rush like cryptocurrency. It all combines to make you feel empty and stuck.

The Method can help you unlock success and happiness by breaking through the barriers of mental overload, anxiety, and procrastination. The Method is incredibly simple, yet understanding the reasoning and process behind it, along with the details that go into it, is essential to making the most of it. Without them, it will just be like any other self-improvement book you read, try, and give up on. Instead, let it be the start of your transformation. The very fact that you're reading this book is proof that The Method works - I never thought I could start writing a book, let alone finish one. If you're willing to give it a shot, you can be more successful and happier than ever before. Today is the perfect day to start, so let's get started!

The

METHOD

VILIUS KOMSKIS

TABLE OF CONTENTS

DEDICATION

To all those who are willing to improve themselves and the world around them.

The METHOD

procrastination
uncertainty
indecision
fear

CHAPTER ONE

WHY YOU FAIL

There are many reasons why you fail or never start in the first place. It may seem easier to ignore these reasons or pretend they don't exist. However, knowing your weaknesses can actually be your greatest strength. Sun Tzu, the author of the *Art of War*, said it best: "If you know the enemy and know yourself, you need not fear the result of a hundred battles. If you know yourself but not the enemy, for every victory gained, you will also suffer a defeat. If you know neither the enemy nor yourself, you will succumb in every battle."

It's equally as important to know ourselves as it is the enemy. More often than not, the enemy *is* ourselves. We're the ones who set ourselves up for failure. Just as we would use our enemy's weaknesses against them in a battle, we need to do the same against ourselves. Let's take a look at the most common reasons why we fail.

One of the most common reasons is **procrastination**. Procrastination is not just "being lazy." Think about a time where you had something weird going on with your health. A strange mole. A cough that lasted way longer than it should have. A headache that didn't go away. You knew it was something you should check out. It was directly impacting you in the most immediate way possible. It was affecting the most important thing in your life, yourself. Yet, you put off going to the doctor until it went away, or it became an emergency that left you no choice but to act. Were you just being lazy? The answer is actually more complex.

THE METHOD

Most of us have learned that, if we ignore potential problems, things might go bad, but they usually don't. We learned that things will most likely work themselves out. It's not only the easiest solution, but it's one that works most of the time. It's a habit. It's very similar to the Schrodinger's Cat paradox. This paradox was proposed by Austrian physicist Erwin Schrödinger in 1935 and is used to illustrate the strange behavior of subatomic particles. In the experiment, a cat is placed in a box with a device that has a 50% chance of killing the cat. According to quantum mechanics, until the box is opened and the cat's fate is known, the cat is both alive and dead at the same time. Until we go to the doctor, we shelter ourselves from the truth that something could be more serious. Diagnosing it might just confirm the bad news. Why risk it?

And thus, however illogically, we convince ourselves that not going is the better choice. Another reason is that we are creatures of habit. Every day we have the same loop of actions that we take. We use every bit of our energy on sustaining this loop, however inefficient some of those actions may be. Working a visit to the doctor into this loop might seem very difficult.

I've used an example of possible health problems, but people procrastinate with work, and social obligations as well. Whatever task there is, there is someone who has procrastinated doing it. Whether it's buying new underwear or planning a funeral, someone has put it off for later. Of course, there are some situations where procrastination gives way. The arch-nemesis of procrastination is urgency. A surgeon won't procrastinate whether he should perform surgery on a dying patient or not. Likewise, a student won't procrastinate writing an essay when there are 2 hours left to submit it or fail. So deadlines or pressure might seem like good options to stop procrastination. But the problem is that you can't always simulate those circumstances to get yourself going. And even if you could, facing a constant stream of urgent situations would cause us a great deal of distress and likely impact the way we perform on these tasks.

Procrastination is why businesses lose millions of dollars every day. It is why you have not achieved or even attempted to achieve things you always dreamed of. Until I developed The Method, I was always stuck in a loop of getting a new idea, being excited about it, starting it, and giving up. Sometimes, I gave up on it before I even started it. It seemed like there was an insurmountable gap between the moment when I got the idea and what I wanted to achieve. I just didn't know enough. I didn't have enough time. I didn't have enough money. And I admit, sometimes, I was too lazy.

If you procrastinate a lot, you're not alone. Even some people known for accomplishing a lot have faced this problem. Tenzin Gyatso, better known as the 14th Dalai Lama, is one such person. He's a spiritual leader who travels around the world advocating for Tibetan people, tirelessly promoting compassion, peace, and freedom. But before this great title and mission, Gyatso started out as many of us do: a bored student, struggling to find motivation. "Only in the face of a difficult challenge or an urgent deadline would I study and work without laziness," the Dalai Lama admitted. [2]

Another is the famous French author Victor Hugo, the author of famous masterpieces like *Les Misérables,* who was also prone to procrastination. To deal with it, he devised a curious solution. Sources state that Hugo once instructed his servant to strip him naked and hide his clothes until he had finished writing a chapter. [3] According to his wife's memoir, that wasn't the only time he did that. Another time, Hugo purchased a huge grey knitted shawl. He used it to wrap himself from head to toe and locked his clothes away. This way, he did not have the temptation to go outside and leave his work unfinished. [4]

Frank Lloyd Wright, one of the most iconic American architects, is another. He is often remembered for his unique house designs, one of which is now a National Historic Landmark - Fallingwater. But most people don't know that Wright created his most famous piece of work in just two hours. Edgar Kaufmann Sr., a Pittsburg department store owner, had hired Wright to design a property for him in Pennsylvania. Wright scouted out the land and promised a fantastic design. But Wright never managed to get started on that promise. He procrastinated for nine months. Kauffmann then gave Wright a surprise call and said that he would drop in to check on his progress. Talk about pressure! In the two hours that it took for Kauffman to drive over, Wright drew up the plans, and the rest is history. [5]

Friedrich Schiller, a German poet, philosopher, and literary theorist, praised for tremendous influence over German literature, had his own way of motivation and dealing with procrastination. Johann Goethe, a fellow writer and friend, once dropped by Schiller's house. Unfortunately, Schiller was out, so Goethe decided to stick around and wait. Being the productive writer, Goethe didn't want to waste a second and sat down at his friend's desk to scribble some notes. Suddenly, a strange smell stopped him in his tracks. A peculiar and offensive odor emanated from the room. Goethe investigated and tracked down the source of the smell. He opened the drawer in the desk and found a pile of rotten apples. The smell was so powerful that it made him light-headed. He had to walk to the window to take in some fresh air to recover. Naturally, Goethe was curious how anybody would forget about such an unforgivable odor in their desk. But, Friedrich's wife Charlotte told him that it was no accident. Schiller would let the apples spoil deliberately.

Somehow, this nose-piercing aroma would inspire him to write, and he could not live or work without it. [6]

Often, we find that we need the comfort of a familiar space in order to concentrate and work. Charles Dickens, the highly methodical author responsible for classics such as *A Tale of Two Cities* and *Oliver Twist*, came up with his own solution to help him focus. He would carry a collection of familiar objects, such as bronze figures of two toads dueling. He would carefully arrange them on his desk when traveling. [7][8] It was only one, seemingly insignificant, detail of his methodical routine, but it was highly effective in making a foreign space feel familiar. Establishing a routine or a comfortable space before starting work is a great way to jumpstart your brain into a creative or productive state.

Sometimes, procrastination can be dangerous, as learned by one Colonel Rall. He was a German commander of the Hessian Troops at the Battle of Trenton. The battle is now considered a turning point in the American War of Independence. On Christmas night, in 1776, George Washington planned a surprise attack on the Hessian forces and crossed the Delaware River. The story goes that a local loyalist handed Rall a note actually warning him of the attack in advance. But, Rall was playing cards that night and wanted to finish the game, and he put the message in his pocket. The next morning, Washington's attack captured most of the Hessian forces, who were still asleep and hungover, with few American losses. Rall himself was shot and died a few hours later. The note warning him of the attack was found in his coat pocket, unopened. [9]

Leonardo Da Vinci is often referred to as a genius from the Italian Renaissance. Undoubtedly, Da Vinci has contributed some of the most influential works of all time. He made significant contributions in nearly every field from botany to art. He made plans and drawings for machines way ahead of his time, such as helicopters and submarines. Yet, it's often left out that Da Vinci never finished anything on time. He was easily distracted. He seemingly "wasted" his talents on sketches and projects that he would never finish. One of the works that he is best remembered for, the *Mona Lisa*, took him 16 years to finish. It took him another 13 years to complete the *Virgin of the Rocks*, which today is in London's National Gallery. Others, such as *The Adoration of the Magi* and *Jerome in the Wilderness*, were never finished.

As a matter of fact, Da Vinci only finished the famous painting *The Last Supper* after the Duke of Milan threatened to cut off funding. When confronted about his delays to the piece, Da Vinci exclaimed that he could not find the perfect face for the villain. He threatened to use the face of the complainer instead if he could not find one. [10]

Later in life, Leonardo regretted for "never having completed a single work." He was also quoted as saying: "Tell me if anything ever was done. Tell me if anything was done." [11] Whether a perfectionist, a procrastinator, or likely both, Da Vinci shared some flaws with all of us.

Procrastination is a common problem you're likely dealing with, but another thing holding you back is **indecision**. Did you ever have a friend offer you two different restaurants to go to and all you had to do was pick one? You likely passed off the decision to your friend. Or you spent time analyzing the two restaurants to see if they will be a good fit and imagine how the night will play out. Or try to find a reason why not pick one of them. And sometimes when you spent too much time thinking about the options, you decided not to go anywhere at all. This is just an example, but you face these micro-decisions hundreds of times throughout your day. And if you are highly analytical like me, you'll find that even the smallest decisions can be exhausting. Obsessing over them will prevent you from starting what you love.

Think about it: if you can't even make a decision about which ice cream to buy, what will you do when you have to pick a university to attend? How will you decide what to write a book on? How will you decide if you want to spend the rest of your life with a particular person? Indecision is scary and dangerous. It's like sitting at the train station, watching the trains stop and go, dithering over where you want to go until the sun sets and all the trains have left. But not making a decision is, in fact, making a decision. It's often a bad decision that can trap us in the same place, or even lead us back to a path that we worked hard to escape. It prevents us from moving forward and getting to where we need to be. So make a decision, even if it's with a coin-flip, and see it through. You can live without regret knowing that you didn't wait for all the trains to leave.

Another thing holding some of you back is **commitment**. Committing to something feels like sticking your feet into quicksand. The more we struggle, the more it swallows us, until we're in too deep to get out. It's scary. Trust me, I get it. I used to stand in the cereal aisle for 10 minutes, trying to pick one. And that's just breakfast cereal. I think in horror about how many other decisions I wasted a lot of time on. The funny thing is, in the end, when you spend that much time analyzing, you either end up not making a decision or making a random one anyway. You'd be better off making a random decision in the first place and saving yourself the stress and time.

That is not to say that sometimes carefully weighing your decisions won't result in a much better outcome. But there are limits to what we can determine through analysis. Yet, sometimes we stress about deciding between two doors when we don't know what's behind either. Like procrastination, commitment issues stem from something deeper. They often stem from bad experiences in the past, where something had a lasting negative impact on our life. Another reason for avoiding commitment is FOMO: the fear of missing out. We don't want to make a decision and find out that the other choice would have resulted in something better.

Finally, there's **failure**. We are our own worst critics. We don't want to be hypocrites, and we don't want to look in the mirror and admit our failures, so we often shy away from things we're worried we can't do. If we don't start that diet that we wanted to try, we won't give up a week into it and have to feel worse than before we started. If we don't try to realize our childhood dream of being an actor, we won't have to tell ourselves later how stupid we were for even thinking we could do it. And we certainly won't have others shaming us further. Facing the prospect of failure is tough. But since you don't know what lies behind door A or door B, you have to take a chance with the information at your disposal.

Have the confidence to walk through either door and embrace all the beautiful failures and successes that may come from your choice. Too many of us live in regret without having explored what lies behind either door.

Another excuse you may have for transforming your life is the lack of **time**. If you only had more time. You could learn how to play the guitar, dance, spend more time with your family and pursue your dreams, if you just had a little extra time to spare. It's the ultimate excuse. After all, we only have so much time in a day. In reality, what you want is not more time. It's better time management and the ability to prioritize. Laura Vanderkam, the author of *168 Hours: You Have More Time Than You Think*, made a good point: "Instead of saying 'I don't have time,' try saying 'it's not a priority,' and see how that feels." It may surprise you to know how much time you waste each day on things that don't matter. You can actually check your phone to see how much time you spend looking at your phone and browsing through the lives of others. You are mostly busy because you don't optimize your time. For example, take out the 15-30 minutes each morning that you browse your phone. Dedicate those 15-30 minutes to learning a new language. After a year, that adds up to 182.5 hours. Do you think you could pick up a thing or two in that amount of time?

But I understand. I was in the same situation as you are. You'll learn in later chapters why we only have a limited amount of real effort we can put in each day. Our mundane jobs, lack of motivation, and neglecting our needs are all to blame for us craving some brain-dead time. When was the last time you woke up eager to conquer the day, wishing you had more time to do something because you were so excited about it? Believe it or not, that mindset is achievable. I've met many people throughout my life who always seemed to be busy. It was first because of school, then work, family, and all the other things in between. Those people never stopped being busy. While they may have gotten ahead in their careers, they missed out on other things, like traveling, experiences, learning, friends, and personal growth. Their mindset seems to be "work hard now, have fun later." The problem with this mindset is that you assume your situation will be better later on than it is now. That you'll still have your health, and frankly speaking, that you'll be alive to have that fun you've been postponing.

It's true what they say: when we are young, we have our health and time, but we don't have money. When we are adults, we have money, we have our health, but we don't have time. When we are old, we have time, we have money, but we don't have our health. If you keep on waiting to live, you'll likely never be in a place where you have all three. Our limited time on this earth is our greatest gift. It reminds us that life is for living now.

I am not saying you should neglect your career and job. This book and The Method are about **balancing** your life. You can do many things at once and adjust your life in real-time, depending on your needs. And that's what The Method will do for you. You'll see what you need to be happy now and how to get ahead.

The excuse of time goes hand in hand with the excuse of money. You may not always have enough money to pay your rent. You have to work two jobs to make ends meet. So why am I going on about learning to play the guitar or pursuing your dreams? It's true that being poor is incredibly challenging and draining. Poverty in itself is an incredibly complex issue with many layers. You have to work twice as much, to get a fraction of something that someone else gets. You can't afford good quality food and healthcare, so that takes a toll down the line. You can't buy quality products, so they break quickly and end up costing more. When you're poor, it's tough to break out of the cycle. You won't spend any extra money you get saving, paying back your debt, or investing in bettering your life. You spend mostly on things to temporarily help you escape your situation. Maybe it's a night out in a bar, ordering takeout, or buying something nice. It's something to reward yourself for the hard work or to get yourself through another tough week. Any extra time you have, you spend doing something mind-numbing to help you forget your stress. It's a vicious cycle. If money is holding you back, to change your life around, something has to give.

Through tiny changes, it is usually possible to pay back your debt, save money, and move up in life. It is true that money does not bring happiness; it makes some problems go away, but, as the saying goes, "wherever you go, there you are." We do not always need money to be happy. Take Mike Rowe from Dirty Jobs, for example. He traveled across the US and met people from all walks of life, from sewer inspectors to bat biologists and horse inseminators. Despite the often unpleasant nature of their jobs, he found that many of these people were some of the happiest he had ever encountered. They were not necessarily traditionally wealthy or successful, but they had an outlook on life that made them happy.

If you're serious about transforming your life, you must have an intense, unwavering desire to do so. Without that passionate commitment, you won't be able to make it happen. I could provide you with an elaborate plan for overcoming your financial problems in a year, but let's face it, you probably wouldn't do it.

Luckily, I'm not going to give you some "magic solution" that you can ignore; instead, I'm here to provide a simple method. All you have to do is commit to completing small, manageable tasks every day. Taking action is imperative if you truly want this to become a reality. Start budgeting and living within your means. Devote some of your day to things that matter and benefit you. Doing this will give you the freedom to reach your goals and create the life you desire. Whatever situation you are now, remember that there someone's been in a worse situation who persevered and got out of it:

Born to a poor family in Hungary in 1874, a young boy had to beg for money on the streets to help his family survive. At eight years old, he took up jobs as a shoe shiner and newspaper salesman. At age 17, he went on the road and began his career as a performer. For the next eight years, he would struggle with poverty. At age 19, his wife had to purchase the $2 marriage certificate as he could not afford it. Five years later, after a performance, his diary would read, "Rained hard. No dinner." In 1898, now a man, he would offer up his act that he spent nearly a decade polishing for $10. There were no takers. He was ready to give up show business for good. You may know this man. His name was Harry Houdini, one of the greatest escape artists that ever lived and one of the most creative minds of the 20th century. Houdini later said, "The greatest escape I ever made was when I left Appleton, Wisconsin."

A girl was born to a teenage single mother and raised in extreme poverty in inner-city Milwaukee. She recalls having to wear overalls made from potato sacks, which prompted other kids to nickname her "Sack Girl." She not only had to deal with extreme poverty but also endure years of physical and sexual abuse. She was raped at the age of 9. At age 14, she became pregnant and had her son die during infancy. [12] Surely, no one could overcome these circumstances and live to be a functioning person. But she did. Oprah Winfrey was the girl's name. She is now a media mogul worth $3 billion and an inspiration to millions. [13]

Having a few gigs fall through, a new comedian found himself homeless. He would spend the next three years living in his 1976 Ford Tempo while showering in gas stations and public swimming pool showers. This man is Steve Harvey, one of the most famous TV show personalities around. And he's not the only famous person to be homeless. Some other people who struggled with homelessness you may know are Dr. Phil, Halle Berry, Suze Orman, Daniel Craig, Ella Fitzgerald, Chris Gardner, and others. [69]

Bottom line? Lack of money is not your excuse.

Finally, there's **effort**. It took me a long time to get this, but we only have a limited number of effort points. Think of life as a video game: in every game your character has health, power, or other bar that prevents the character from performing unlimited actions. But for some reason, we don't seem to realize that we have these limits too. Every day you have a finite amount of effort to which you can devote your complete mental or physical focus.

Our bodies get tired, and our minds do too. Take any one of your days. Imagine you don't do anything important. You don't write the novel you wanted, you don't go to basketball practice, and you don't have a business meeting with your employees. Instead, you do tasks that seemingly don't require that much mental OR physical effort. You go to the store, walk in the park, sit on the couch, and watch Netflix. At the end of the day, are you still feeling energized? No. Somehow, your energy is not there. Although you "took it easy," you still spent your effort, and didn't restore your energy. You see, whether you notice or not, even the most mediocre and lazy tasks can use up your effort points.

Paradoxically, some of the things that we think consume energy can actually give us more effort points. Think of working out, walking, and meditating. They are all tasks that seem like they would drain us. But research shows they can actually give us energy and concentration. In turn, they boost our amount of effort points we have throughout the day. The point is, while certain things can boost our effort points, and others drain them, we only have a limited number of them. We have to be methodical in how we use them throughout the day. That's why sitting on the couch can feel comfy and restful at first, but will lead to all your effort points drained. It will also make you unlikely to do anything else.

Motivation is a tool that people try to summon in their moments of weakness. They imagine that motivation is like a bolt of lightning. Maybe an inspirational speech. Reading a success story. A motivational quote. A movie. Anything that will give them the spark they need to get up, go, and keep going. But just like a bolt of lightning, motivation comes and goes quickly, lighting things up for a moment but vanishing in moments. Motivation is unpredictable and unreliable in the long run. It doesn't transform you.

You will continue to keep waiting for a day when the weather is good. For when you feel rested. For when you feel happy. For all the stars to align. Powerful motivation comes from powerful emotions. Often from tragic events in your life. A heartbreak. Loss of a loved one. Prospect of losing something that holds you together. These events can break you apart or give you the drive to succeed. It's when you have no more safety nets, and you want to succeed as much as you want to take your next breath. That's the only real type of motivation that is sustainable. But it's not something that you can summon, nor do you want to. The average person doesn't need to save their marriage, their life, or survive homelessness. The average person struggles to get out of bed in the morning. Doing their work. Pursuing a passion. Doing something that needs to be done. They are not heroic tasks by any means, but they still require focus and mental energy, regardless.

As epic as social media makes our lives appear, it's not picture-worthy moments that make up our days. It's the little tasks that we repeat, which push us forward and make us succeed. So how do we do that? How do we push forward? Preachers, influencers, and gurus will tell you that "all you need is the right mindset." That's part of it. But I want to provide you with a tangible and methodical approach that will work in the long run.

This is where The Method comes in. It will help you understand your needs and give you the fuel to improve every day. If you think about your most productive days of your life, you either were under pressure, or you simply felt energetic. Mentally and physically. And that's what you'll strive for. You'll develop the right mindset. When we feel good, we do the right things without any excuses. The Method will teach you to become a relentless and highly methodical beast.

CONCLUSION:

Knowing your weakness can be your greatest strength. Understand why you fail and overcome excuses that prevent you from moving forward.

Things I want to do
Jenuary 15
MOM

CHAPTER TWO

THE METHOD

A time-tested method for increasing productivity is the legendary to-do list. It has been around as long as people have. Ben Franklin, a famously productive man, used a variation of to-do lists for self-improvement. In 1726, according to his autobiography, he drafted a thirteen-week plan to seek a more virtuous living. [14] He practiced virtues such as resolution, temperance, frugality, sincerity, etc. He would practice each of the virtues for a period of one week. He had a chart with each of the virtues and a column that had the days of the week.

Each evening, he would recall his day and put a dot for each fault he committed. After the 13 weeks, he would start the process all over again. In one year, he would be able to commit four cycles. This system made him so happy that he decided to continue this for the rest of his life. Lists are a great way to visually keep track of and plan what you need to accomplish that day. It takes the stress away from having to remember all the tasks and is generally great to improve work productivity. But, in my personal experience, I have found that I have a hard time adhering to a to-do list. It has the opposite effect for me.

As an entrepreneur and freelancer, time management is crucial. But working for myself offers freedom and flexibility. A to-do list can be rigid, stressful, and sometimes, straight-up menacing. The same reason why it's helpful can also be the reason why it's not. Staring at a list that displays what must be done that day is not always pleasant – specially when you fail to complete it. Sometimes, I simply don't want to make a to-do list. It's so formal. It's boring. It's not motivating enough. That's part of the reason why I developed my own method.

I realized that the classic list failed to address many ingredients that make my day productive and joyful. The issue was not even the to-do list itself, but rather my perspective about it. A to-do list only addresses our chores, our work, and things we otherwise dread. But after I took a step back and examined what made me happy and productive, I realized with surprise that it was a lot more than the chores and work.

For example, I found that a big part that was missing from my life as someone who works from home was socializing. While I love my alone time, I isolate myself from people for most of the day. What if on my list I added social things like calling my friends or family? Or making myself go to an event? It's not something you'd typically find on a normal person's to-do list. But we should consider it. After that, I started thinking of other categories that I need to fill up each day to maximize my well-being as well as my productivity. Things like self-improvement, spending time outdoors, dedicating time for personal projects, and more. I realized the best list was a combination of about six different categories.

Let's think of ourselves as a vehicle for a second. For too long we have only planned our route and where we need to go. But what about what actually makes the car run? The gas, oil, coolant, and all the different parts. If we neglect these things, one broken part can set off a chain reaction that can make driving difficult or bring the vehicle to a complete standstill. The same goes for us. A to-do list is only a map with basic directions. Every day, we need to bring our attention to everything that moves us forward in life, not just the basics. We have to dig deeper to understand what makes us productive, feel fulfilled, let us grow and be happy.

The Method is one of the easiest additions to your life. Put simply, *The Method is a daily planner that includes the things you need to do in order to live a happy, productive life.*

It will have the most profound effect. It's straightforward. You'll create a categorized daily planner that considers all the things that make your life happy. You will write "things I want to do" and the day's date on top. You will analyze which categories make your life fulfilling. Then, every day, you fill these categories with tasks based on your current needs.

But it's not just a wish list: there are specific categories you need to include, and as mentioned earlier, it's very important to understand the reasoning behind each type of category and the method itself. That's all there is to The Method and the extent of effort that it requires. In the following pages, you'll learn the reasoning behind this method. I will tell you why it can and will work for you. I've tried other types of to-do lists, organizers, apps, and tricks, all to no avail. The Method is the one that worked for me. It can work for you too.

To get started, all you need is a whiteboard and a marker. You can also use a notebook, your phone, or anything else that you use to plan your time. But I found that using a big whiteboard is the most effective for me since I can clearly see what I want to do that day. I can also glance at it at any time easily from any spot in the room. When I leave my house or office, that's when I transfer it into my notebook.

Get started by writing "**Things I want to do**" on the top left. Why precisely that phrase? Many people start their day by writing "To do," "chores", "tasks," "shopping list." How much do you look forward to things that sound like that? It is the wrong mindset to start with, and it calibrates your brain into a work attitude. Unless you really love your work, it will make you dread the day to even write a list like that. Every day you wake up, you should be in charge of your day. This time is yours and no one else's. By writing "things I *want* to do," you are letting yourself know that *you control* what happens today, and these are things that you actually want to do. And The Method is unique because you will plan out other areas of your life, not just chores.

Next, write **today's date** on the top right. There's no fancy reason other than a reminder that each day is a new start. Take a photo of your list and take it on the go. This is a pleasant way to start, instead of jumping straight to the categories.

Finally, we have the most crucial part of this method. You will **determine which categories in your life matter the most to you.** You will figure out what makes your day great and your life fulfilling. You will make columns with each of these categories at the top. This includes not only your work, but things that have to do with your health, emotional well-being, and self-development. These categories are what you will fill up every day.

Sometimes, one category will be fuller than another. Sometimes a category may be entirely blank. Every day, your needs, mood, and life circumstances will fluctuate. Your chart should reflect that. Think of the categories as cups. Full cups equal a happy you. As they get drained, you will fill them up. When most of your cups are full, you can focus on the ones that need refilling. It is when we neglect the empty cups that everything starts falling apart.

CONCLUSION:

Grab a marker and a whiteboard, and start methodically engineering a better life for yourself!

CHAPTER THREE

FIND YOUR INGREDIENTS TO HAPPINESS

Let's take a look at the categories that I found crucial in creating a beautiful environment within myself and around me. These are the right categories for me, but your priorities may vary a little. I'll also cover some other categories that you may want to consider for your own personalized planner.

MONEY

This issue is a top concern for nearly anyone, no matter what your income level. Chapman University surveyed 1,190 adults across the United States. They asked them 94 questions related to personal anxieties, environment, government, and crime. From this survey, they compiled a list of the top 10 fears of 2018. In fourth place, 57% of people reported being afraid or very afraid of "not having enough money for the future." Which just edged out "people I love dying," a fear shared by 56% of people. "High medical bills" was the 10th most feared with 53%. [15] Conduct any study you wish, and you will find that American or not, rich or poor, people are predominantly preoccupied with fears about their financial security. We are obsessed about attaining it, keeping it, or getting ourselves out of a jam.

While money was never and is currently not the main focus in my life, I am not oblivious about the fact that I need money to survive. Every day, I write down things in this category that are related to my work and different things that can generate money and pay the bills. Aside from your work tasks, money management and saving can also be in this category. Debt can put immense pressure on your life, and, left unmanaged, can create a boatload of problems down the line. Doing little tasks every day that will help you manage spending and bring you out of debt can be incredibly helpful.

CAREER

Most people think about their immediate job and its duties, but I find it important to look further ahead. Areas where you can grow, push yourself, and pursue your dreams. Are you pursuing the line of work you really want to do? In this category, I put down things that get me closer to my ideal career. Perhaps you are working a job you don't like and you always knew you wanted to be a radio host. A daily task could be scouting what experience you need or writing a tailored resume for that job. Something to get you started. Every day, you will move closer and closer to that goal. Soon enough, you will be working as a radio host. Or maybe you'll end up on a surprising new path, or get that promotion you always wanted. We tend to get sucked into the immediate demands of a project or job and neglect to plan where we really want to be. This category is an opportunity to think outside the box and move closer to a job you always wanted.

SELF-IMPROVEMENT

This category is crucial and often one that I tend to neglect. It is simple: what can I do today to improve myself? Perhaps reading a few pages of a book. Ten minutes of learning another language. Learning one chord on the guitar. Spending a few minutes to meditate. It is when we stay stagnant or decline that we start feeling inadequate and lack self-confidence. Thanks to The Method, over the last few years, I've acquired a heap of new skills and knowledge and have improved my body. I didn't become a musician, but I picked up the guitar for the first time in my life and learned a song. I didn't become a bodybuilder, but I can now do 15 pull-ups easily. I didn't master Spanish, but I learned enough to understand a basic conversation. I didn't become Buddha, but I started meditating and learned to calm down – and as a result, I sleep better and stress less.

Tiny things, done regularly, can add up to something awesome in the end. These things by themselves will lead you into paths and circles that you have never dreamed of being in. The founder of the martial art of Aikido, Morihei Ueshiba, often referred to as the "Great Teacher," said it best: "Life is growth. If we stop growing, technically and spiritually, we are as good as dead." Even Einstein was convinced of this: "Once you stop learning, you start dying". Learning changes the actual physical structure of our brain. [16] It organizes and reorganizes your brain.[17]

SOCIAL

Ever since I was 12, I've spent most of my time at my computer and staying inside. At first it was because I didn't have many friends after moving to the US. Then, it was because my work was all online. For whatever reason, I always found myself comfortable inside my home. However, it took me nearly 16 years to realize that a lot of the time I actually felt bored, lonely, and otherwise lacking social interactions. My social life was completely unpredictable. I didn't understand that this was a big part of my happiness and that I needed to take charge in that area.

So as of a year ago, I made it a priority to find a way to be social every single day. Whether it is to simply call a relative or friend, send a video message to someone I haven't spoken to in a while, or even play a basketball pickup game, I work something into my daily planner. As a result, I no longer find myself feeling depressed or lonely because I didn't see anyone or because I didn't receive any texts. It doesn't matter if you are an extrovert or an introvert – you can't neglect this essential category.

If you are an introvert, you can use this category to slowly push yourself to talk to people and get out there. It will help you, and it will help your business as well. It is easy to "socialize" with social media, but it is crucial to do it in person as well. More importantly, a strong social support system will actually help you to live longer [18] and allow you to get up when you are down.

NATURE & OUTDOORS

Another thing that took me a while to get is that nature was a big part of my life. Someone once told me that it is only when we get older that we start to really appreciate nature, and I think in a way that's true. As a civilization, we have disconnected from nature due to our giant cities and technology. There's a reason why a walk in nature reduces your anxiety and stress. Researchers found that walking encourages the release of endorphins in your brain. Walking also sends pressure waves from your feet through your arteries and increases blood flow to the brain. [19] Combine that with the soothing sounds and sights of nature, and it becomes easy to see why so many creative geniuses prioritize nature walks.

Einstein walked 1.5 miles to and from Princeton University every day. [20] Charles Darwin took three 45-minute walks a day. [21] Beethoven loved "long, vigorous walks" in which he was known to carry a pencil and blank sheet music. Satie, Tchaikovsky, and Mahler also all knew the power of regularly scheduled mid-day walks. [22] Humans were meant to live together with nature, yet we have long neglected that part. And it's harder to connect with nature than it used to be: it is increasingly hard to find anywhere that isn't polluted with our garbage, sounds, or buildings, especially if you live in a highly urbanized area. But it's super important to do our best and find time to sometimes quite literally hug a tree or stare at the clouds. [23] Founder of the Cloud Appreciation Society and author of The Cloudspotter's Guide, Gavin Pretor-Pinney says, "Having your head in the clouds, even for just a few minutes each day, is good for your mind, good for your body, and good for your soul." [24]

WORLD & OTHERS

One surprising ingredient that's missing from many of our lives is giving. When was the last time you went out of your way to be generous? Done something without self-interest? Without any expectation of reciprocity? If you've helped someone in the past, you know how rewarding giving can be. I know, many of you are thinking one of two things; one is that "I don't have enough time or money myself, how can I give?" 99% of giving doesn't have to involve any money. Sure, it's nice to donate to a fundraising campaign every once in a while, but that's not the only way.

It can be a small gesture like taking a photo for a tourist couple or calling up a friend and asking them if they are okay and if they need any help with anything. Volunteering at an animal shelter. Giving free lessons. Adjusting a business to in some way help our planet.

The second thing you may be thinking is: "how does giving benefit me?" At first, you may think that it is those solely on the receiving end that benefit, but take a deeper look. Taking a photo for someone will result in a smile from a stranger, making you feel good. Listening to a friend or helping them will strengthen your bond with them. Teaching will help you understand your craft better and build your reputation. Volunteering at an animal shelter will teach you compassion and allow you to make a difference in an animal's life. Adjusting your business to help our planet will better your brand's image and make your employees feel like they are making a difference.

Dan Price, the CEO of Gravity Payments, experienced the unexpected results of giving. One of his employees was Haley, a 32-year-old phone tech earning $35,000 a year. Haley was on a smoking break one day seemingly in a bad mood. "Seems like something's bothering you," Price said. "What's on your mind?" He was shocked when Haley replied, "You're ripping me off." Haley was quite shy, so this must've been a topic he had on his mind for a while. "Your pay is based on market rates," Price protested. "If you have different data, please let me know. I have no intention of ripping you off." But the data didn't matter for Haley, who responded with, "I know your intentions are bad. You brag about how financially disciplined you are, but that just translates into me not making enough money to lead a decent life." Price walked away from the conversation hurt. After all, he prided himself on treating his employees well.

It took him a while, but he eventually realized that Haley may have been right – not only about the pay, but also his intentions. "I was so scarred by the recession that I was proactively, and proudly, hurting my staff," Price said. He set out on a mission to tackle income inequality. First, Price started to hand out 20% raises each year to his employees. But that wasn't enough, and soon he tried something unimaginable. He announced he would phase in a $70,000 minimum salary wage for his 120 employees. He even cut his own $1.1 million salary to help cover it. This was unprecedented and frankly, seemed to go against all common sense in economics. After all, if people are willing to work for $35,000, why would you raise their salary to $70,000? Many pundits thought that nothing good could come of this.

But after the *New York Times* covered this announcement, the reaction was overwhelmingly supportive. Over 500 million reactions on social media. Price even received stories from employees in other companies who received raises from their bosses who were inspired by the story. His company was flooded with 4500 new applications in the first week alone. And it wasn't just for people looking for more money: one application was from a 52-year-old Yahoo executive who was willing to take an 80-85% cut to work there. "I spent many years chasing the money," she said. "Now I'm looking for something fun and meaningful." However, it wasn't just positivity that was flowing in. Price got plenty of criticism of how he was a socialist who was bound to fail. But six months after implementing these changes, the company's performance surprised everyone. Revenue growth doubled. Profits doubled. The customer retention rate rose to 95%. [25] All of which seems to go against common sense in economics.

However, what basic economics fails to consider is that *happy workers are productive and loyal workers.* They do more, they lift their peers up, and they have a vested interest in their company's success. The customers feel the effects of this as well.

Being charitable goes beyond business. It has a positive psychological effect. Through millions of years, our brains have evolved to maximize our own chances of survival, so it's baffling to some that we'd help others while incurring personal costs. But today, there's scientific research that proves that giving your talent, time, and money is an incredible way to find fulfillment and happiness. Of course, it is difficult to believe that it's advantageous to be anything but selfish; even with Gravity's proven track record, for example, there are business people today who remain incredulous and critical of their approach. It seems logical to many that selfishness is the best way to succeed, but research suggests the opposite.

At a very basic level, because of how fragile our offspring are, the survival of our species depends on our care for those in need. But what about "Survival of the Fittest" by the great Charles Darwin? Most people think his theory says the opposite. But in fact, Darwin talks about benevolence nearly 100 times in his seminal book *Descent of Man*. His conclusion is that sympathy, love, and cooperation is present in the animal world as well. Darwin includes many examples of this in the book. In one such instance, "a young pelican, carried away by a strong stream, was guided and encouraged in its attempts to reach the shore by half a dozen old birds." Crows demonstrated similar behavior: "Mr. Blyth, as he informs me, saw Indian crows feeding two or three of their companions which were blind." [26]

In 2008, a bottlenose dolphin rescued two beached whales and led them to safe waters in New Zealand. A group of swimmers who witnessed this saw the dolphin circling around the whales tightly and splashing everywhere. They thought that this was aggressive behavior towards the whales, but it turns out, the dolphin was warding off sharks. [27] There was another case where a leopard killed a mother baboon and found a 1-day old baboon. Instead of killing it, she took care of the baby baboon for hours, at one point saving it from a pack of hyenas. [28] Unfortunately the baboon did not survive the night without the nurture of its mother, but the leopard did spare her from a worse death.

So we know altruism is present in nature. But how does it affect our human brains? Studies like the one in 2006 by Grafman and Moll have shown that giving activates a primitive part of the brain that usually responds to food or sex. [29] As Jenny Santi, the author of *The Giving Way to Happiness,* puts it, "altruism, the experiment suggests, is not a superior moral faculty that suppresses basic selfish urges; rather, it is hard-wired in the brain and pleasurable". [30]

The final aspect of giving is that it has an exponential effect. We often hear stories where a simple smile or compliment at school stopped them from committing suicide. How a pair of shoes kept someone from getting frostbite in the winter. How a compliment made someone's day. If you help or be nice to someone, chances are they will do the same to others. I've heard many "pay it forward" stories, where people do something nice for someone and ask them to do something nice for others – for example, when people pay for a toll or a meal for the person behind them.

Now, the receiver could thank them for the nice gesture and that might be the end of it. Which would still be a great conclusion, as you made someone's day. But what usually happens is that person is inspired to pay for the person behind them. And it keeps going. It's a fascinating phenomenon, and one that you can try yourself. Everyone gains something. Everyone becomes a tiny bit happier. Now take the opposite; do something negative – will it not spread like a disease?

You may think to yourself; "I don't have enough myself, how can I give?" It's often those who have the least, that give the most.

CREATIVITY

We are all born creative; it is only as we get older that we lose our creativity and willingness to experiment. Everyone can nurture their creativity and deepen their understanding and curiosity. However, our educational system and jobs fill us with concrete processes and facts, which stifle our creativity. We tend to reward those who follow, fit in, and don't question our methods. We also fear failure and readily shame ourselves or anyone else who makes mistakes, making taking creative risks seem unappealing. Yet, it is our failures that offer the best learning opportunities; it is often our mistakes that lead to the greatest discoveries, as they take us off the beaten path.

Innovative companies like Google have embraced failure as part of their company culture. In Google's main campus in Mountain View, California, is a secret laboratory namd Google X. It's referred to as the "moonshot factory." Here, engineers and inventors are encouraged to work on extremely ambitious ideas. The goal for any project of the X lab is to make a problem 10 times better within 10 years. One such problem is millions of people dying on the roads each year due to car crashes. One science fiction solution that the lab came up with was to create driverless cars that don't crash. Google's autonomous car is now a reality, and it has driven over 20 million testing miles already; this technology may transform the world. Google helped make this and other programs a success was through embracing and rewarding failure. Edward Teller, the "Captain of Moonshots," says, "You must reward people for failing. If not, they won't take risks and make breakthroughs. If you don't reward failure, people will hang on to a doomed idea for fear of the consequences. That wastes time and saps an organization's spirit." [31]

Creative experiences and learning have a huge impact on my overall happiness. We all have secret goals, such as mastering the piano, trying our hand at pottery, becoming fluent in another language, launching a business, or writing a book. Yet, these goals often remain idle until we completely give up on them. However, with The Method and a bit of accountability, you can make these creative goals visible once more and start finding the time to make them a reality. You have already taken the first step, just by envisioning what you want to create or learn.

CONCLUSION:

Figure out the ingredients to your happiness.

45

My
Method

CHAPTER FOUR

HOW IS THE METHOD DIFFERENT?

In the mid-1800s, over 300,000 prospectors from around the world rushed to California as news of gold discovery broke out. People wanted a shot at striking it rich, often risking their lives just to make it to the Gold Coast. The consequences of the gold rush were severe for most, with many losing their life savings or even their lives. Entire populations of native people were driven out of their homes. Over 100,000 Native Americans died of starvation, homicide, and disease during the gold rush. Landscapes were devastated and rivers choked with sediment. Very few people actually struck gold. And most of the people who earned the most during the rush weren't even digging for nuggets. They were the people who sold picks and shovels to all the prospectors. As Mark Twain famously said, "When everybody is digging for gold, it's good to be in the pick and shovel business."

Fast forward: nearly 200 years later, the same applies to our society today. Gurus, experts, millionaires, all claim that they struck gold and "you can too!" The only thing that changed is that the shovels have been replaced with books, courses, and seminars. There are thousands of YouTube videos claiming that you can make $50, $100, $1000, even $10,000 a day! Ironically, the very same people don't make the bulk of their money from the methods they promote. They're selling materials and videos to other people to learn the methods – in other words, they're making their money from selling the shovels. Two centuries later, it still pays to be in the pick and shovel business.

So how is The Method different? Is it just another attempt to do the same? Why would The Method work when other methods, diets, and courses have failed you in the past? Am I just trying to sell you a new shovel?

If you want to make a lot of money, there are thousands of books by people who became millionaires, sharing their secrets to success. Some world-renowned chefs reveal their secret recipes and methods. There are diet plans by people who lost 200 pounds and are now in the best shape of their life. So, in theory, if you follow their exact footsteps, you should be able to reach similar success, right? But that's rarely the case. Why? Because that's the path that worked for them in their unique circumstances. We are all different, and none of our lives are the same. A lot of things have to come together, including a little bit of luck, to get to where they are.

Take a simple recipe. Have you ever seen an awesome-looking cake and tried to make it yourself? You followed the recipe to the dot yet came out with something that looks like it's been through a rough road trip in the trunk of your car. That's because the creator may possess skills and experience that you don't have. Oftentimes, these recipes, plans, and books, leave out small details that turn out to be crucial ingredients in their success. A millionaire may explain how they achieved their success – but leave out the part where their parents left them a $250,000 inheritance.

If any person out there has a golden opportunity, you can be sure that they won't share it with you until they squeeze every last bit out of it. But let's say you are an author with pure intentions of helping people make money. The very act of revealing your exact methods may destroy any money-making opportunity they offer. What business works today, may be overcrowded and ineffective by tomorrow. But what about diets, self-help books, and other things that can be revealed to the masses without sacrificing anything? For those, there are only two ways to make them. Make them tailored to a broad audience, as general as possible, or share specifically what worked for you. With either option, the reader and their unique needs are left out.

The Method is different because it is a tool tailored to your own unique needs and goals. I'm providing the framework, but you decide how to fill it in. With just a few minutes each day, you'll determine exactly what you're lacking or striving for that day. By addressing these needs, and filling those cups, you will become more happy, successful, and fulfilled. It's a domino effect, with the pieces falling in the right direction. After using The Method for a while, you will notice a fundamental shift in your thinking, and your perspective and outlook on life will change. It's a big claim for a method that is in reality a simple chart…but it's true.

You won't be following someone's one-off success story – not even mine! The Method forces you to build your own good habits and teaches you to delve within to see what you're truly lacking. It's not time-consuming and won't overcomplicate your life. You will move at your own pace and keep moving. It will help you consistently balance, heal, and improve yourself.

What you need is already within you. Are you more likely to succeed following someone else's plans tailored to them or guide yourself to success at your own pace? What happens when you become your guru is that you learn things along the way, build discipline, and fundamentally change yourself and grow. In contrast, what happens when you follow someone else's path is that you fall behind, get stuck, and fail.

THE METHOD

This method will not provide you with a plan to get rich overnight or how to become a world-renowned chef. But, it will be a tool that allows you to keep moving forward, feel fulfilled, and achieve more than you thought was possible. In the last two years, I was able to start multiple businesses, travel the world, transform my health, and write this book. Among many other incredible things that I thought I'd never do. And for that, I credit The Method.

CONCLUSION:

The Method works where other systems fail because it is tailored to your own unique needs, goals, and pace.

CHAPTER FIVE

HACKING YOUR BRAIN

Understanding the inner workings of your brain, the real process behind your decision-making, is crucial in setting up your path to success. We like to think that we consciously choose our actions and make our decisions. In reality, most of our thought processes occur in the subconscious and unconscious parts of your mind. This is why, for example, we are easily influenced by marketing.

Derren Brown, a well-known mentalist and illusionist, invited a couple of marketing executives to demonstrate just that. Upon their arrival, Brown asked them to design an advertisement poster that included a company name, slogan, and logo for a taxidermy store. Brown gave no other instructions. He also placed an envelope on the table that was to be untouched, with a few design ideas of his own. After half an hour, Brown returned to the room. The execs came up with a bear playing the harp, with the name "Animal Heaven" and the slogan "the best place for dead animals." For the logo, they chose angel wings. It was oddly specific, and probably not something that we'd come up ourselves.

Then, Brown asked them to open the envelope on the table that had remained untouched. Inside was a near-identical poster with a harp-playing bear, the name "Creature Heaven," and the slogan "where the best dead animals go." And angel wings for the logo. How was he able to predict precisely what the two marketing executives would draw? He used the same techniques that advertisers use on people. What Brown had done was carefully curated their journey to his office.

The whole ride leading up to the office was full of symbols, words, and pretty much identical images that would later appear in their poster. They drove past a "London Zoo," walked by a poster of a harp-playing bear, saw a group of children wearing a zoo logo with gates, and even a sign labeled "Creature Heaven." Brown had subtly shown them images that would be useful for the exercise he had planned. He knew that, just like we do every day, they would register these images subconsciously, and then without knowing, these images would insert themselves into their thought process.

This was obviously a carefully planned trick that only a world-class mentalist like Derren Brown can pull off. But every day, we fall for the very same trick ourselves. Brands spend millions of dollars to weave their slogans and images into our environments and our heads. It could be an ad that we skipped before a video, a billboard that we drove past or a post that we scrolled through on social media. Those fractions of a second add up over time. Even if they fail to capture our full attention, they get stored unconsciously. Consequently the next time we see their products, we feel a strange familiarity, and without knowing why, we're more likely to buy them. But these techniques are used for much more than selling you a teeth-whitening kit on social media.

Internet memes, for example, may seem innocent enough until you realize that they are used for more than casual humor. Politicians and corporations actually have teams who produce them to shape your opinion of candidates and issues, and to sway you in their favor. Yet, we share them without realizing their potential intent.

But this is not a book about marketing or politics. I wanted to illustrate how these techniques are used to influence us daily. It's just the way our brains work. But by being aware of these techniques, you can become aware of how you form your opinions and make your decisions. By shining a spotlight in that dark part of your brain, you can start making decisions that, instead of profiting corporations, benefit *you*.

There's a lot that goes on in our heads without our realizing it. Another thing that you should pay attention to, for example, is your habits. Tiny habits dictate your daily behavior. They are an automatic set of actions that you repeat every day. Most of these actions have formed without you even realizing it. Ever wonder why you reach for your phone in the morning?

Our brains are incredibly efficient. Because we are exposed to such a vast amount of information each day, our minds look for patterns and utilize them as shortcuts. Do you remember a time when you were driving, zoned out, and when you looked back, you couldn't recall the last few minutes? Yet somehow, you and the car were still in one piece. You didn't drive into a tree or anything. It's because your brain took over. We use thousands of these mental shortcuts each day. And to be honest, they serve an important purpose: if we didn't, we'd be exhausted and overloaded. These shortcuts are essential to our existence. Yet, some shortcuts are not always beneficial to us. Do any of these seem familiar?...

Sad → eat junk food.

Bored → check phone.

Stressed → smoke a cigarette.

Cute boy/girl → get nervous.

Overwhelmed → procrastinate.

THE METHOD

In 1904, a scientist named Ivan Pavlov received a Nobel Prize for his work in medicine. Pavlov was researching the digestive system using dogs. He discovered something that changed how we understand human behavior.

While measuring the amount of saliva during digestion, he noticed that the dogs were salivating before they even tasted the food. We need saliva to help us chew food and prepare it for digestion. But, it seems that the dogs were triggering this process early. It got weirder as he paired the food with the sound of the bell or the footsteps of the researchers. The dog would start salivating at the sound of the bell or footsteps, even if no food was present. This later became known as classical conditioning.

In the case of the dogs, it worked something like this:

First, you introduce a stimulus, like food. This results in a response – in this case, salivating. Then you pair the stimulus with another one, like the sound of a bell. Which still results in salivation. After a while, you can take away the first stimulus (the food) and the result is still the same. [1]

Stimulus	→ Response
(Food)	(Dogs salivate)
Stimulus 1 + Stimulus 2	→ Response
(Food) (Sound of a bell)	(Dogs salivate)
~~Stimulus 1~~ + Stimulus 2	→ Response
~~(Food)~~ (Sound of a bell)	(Dogs salivate)
Stimulus	→ Response

(Sound of a bell)	(Dogs salivate)

These findings were extraordinary. It means our brains are subconsciously pre-programmed for specific responses. These responses can influence our behavior. Let's take a real-life example. A smoker sees a cigarette (stimulus). He then lights up and smokes the cigarette (response). Later, in addition to the original stimulus of seeing a cigarette, they add another – being bored. The response is still the same, and the smoker lights up the cigarette and smokes it. Eventually, just being bored becomes a sufficient stimulus to trigger the response.

Stimulus → Response
(Seeing a cigarette) (Smoking a cigarette)

Stimulus 1 + Stimulus 2 → Response
(Seeing a cigarette) (Being bored) (Smoking a cigarette)

~~Stimulus 1~~ + Stimulus 2 → Response
~~(Seeing a cigarette)~~ (Being bored) (Smoking a cigarette)

Stimulus → Response
(Being bored) (Smoking a cigarette)

Knowing this, you can analyze a habit you want to get rid of and see if there's a stimulus that triggers it. Then change it. Take control of your brain's tendency to come up with shortcuts, by consciously figuring out what's actually prompting behaviors you want to stop.

Another trick is to use visual and auditory cues to your advantage. Our brain seems to built habits much easier if there are auditory or visual cues associated with them. App creators use this trick on you all the time. One of the reasons why you check social media so often is those little notifications. They come in the form of sounds, lights, or banners. Your phone cheeps or buzzes, and you instinctually open the app to check what's new.

Just like the lights and sounds on a slot machine in a casino, social media is designed to give us a small rush of dopamine every time you open it. But instead of a jackpot, you receive likes. Maybe it's not a coincidence that much like drug dealers, social media refers to its customers as users. Your brain wants to repeat the actions that give you pleasure. And thus, you keep opening the app every time you hear that notification.

The notification is the stimulus – just like that bell Pavlov rang. You can turn off the notifications and interrupt this process. You probably won't check your account as often. But we also check our social media when we are bored or lonely. Next thing you know, being bored or lonely becomes enough to trigger the response of checking your social media. Without the need for the original stimulus…just like Pavlov's dogs.

We can interrupt the cycle of bad habits by cutting out as many triggers as possible. But we perform these actions because they provide some kind of perceived benefit for us. Whether physical or psychological. Thus, those habits are not easily eliminated. More often than not, replacing one habit with another is more effective. For example, every time you get a notification, instead of checking your account, write down an idea in your notes. Over time, the notification will benefit you, instead of the corporations.

You could also use the same technique to reverse engineer something positive into your life. Let's say you set an alarm to go off randomly three times a day. Every time you hear that particular alarm sound, you take a deep breath and relax. Or write one line of a poem. Or meditate for a few minutes. Over time, you will program yourself to do these things without much thinking or effort.

Science also suggests that smaller, precise actions are more likely to result in forming habits. For example, instead of telling yourself that "I will start a diet," you should say something like, "I will eat a bowl of fruit salad each morning." If you want to start exercising, you can take the same approach. Instead of saying, "I will start going to the gym," you could say, "as soon as I get home from work, I will do ten pushups." These small actions are much easier to start because they do not seem as exhausting. They also tend to result in a ripple effect that gradually transforms the rest of your habits.

We also tend to form habits more easily if there is a physical movement associated with it. Let's say you wanted to plan your day out. Thinking about the most important things you want to do that day in the morning could work. But what would work even better is if you associated a physical action with it. For example, the action of taking a marker and writing it out on a whiteboard.

CONCLUSION:

Become aware of your habits and how they form, and you can start changing them.

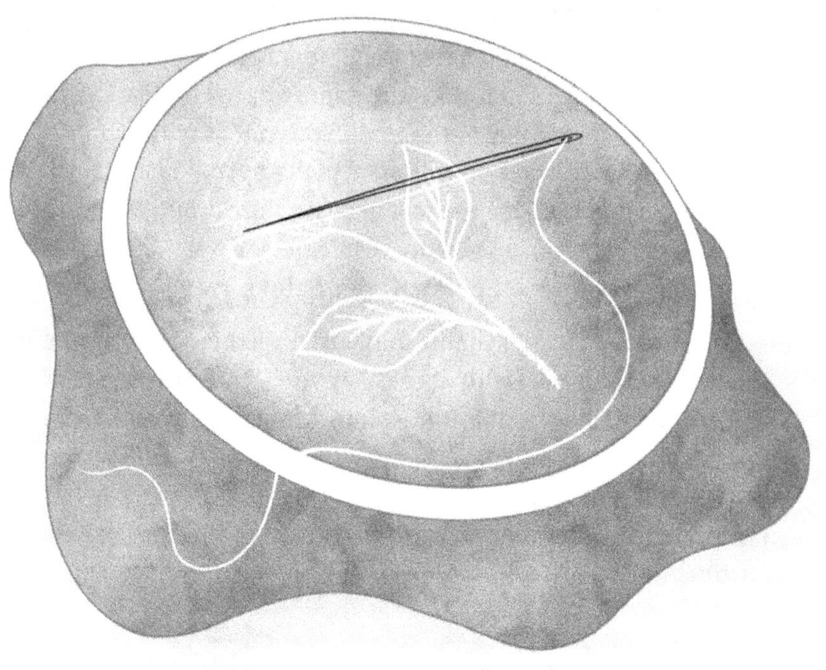

CHAPTER SIX

MAXIMIZE YOUR SUCCESS

There are some people who can start something and see it through till the end. Then there are people who, like me, are great at starting things but rarely finish anything. Finally, there are those who don't even start. Regardless of which type of person you are, you can use these simple rules to make sure you never give up on The Method or yourself.

THE MAGIC OF STARTING

You've come a long way. You not only realized that you can use some help in moving your life forward, but you took the effort to learn about The Method. Now it's the easy part; just start! It is one of the simplest methods you'll come across with the most profound effects.

If you've never started anything, or if you're stuck in a rut, The Method can help you get going. It doesn't matter whether you want to start a new business, get in shape, or write a book – just start taking small actions and see what happens.

One person who almost gave up before getting their start is J.K. Rowling, the author of the Harry Potter series. In an interview, she revealed that she had been close to giving up on her first novel, Harry Potter and the Philosopher's Stone. She was struggling to make ends meet. She was a single mother on welfare, and she had been rejected by dozens of publishers. But she didn't give up; she kept writing, and eventually found a publisher who was willing to take a chance on her. The rest, as they say, is history.

If J.K. Rowling had given up, the world would have missed out on one of the most beloved book series of all time. So, if you're feeling stuck, remember that it's always worth it to just start.

THE POWER OF SMALL STEPS

One of the biggest mistakes people make when using planners is not being specific enough. Before you put something on the board, make sure you break it down into the smallest steps possible. If you put a huge goal like "write a book" on the board, you will inevitably look at this enormous task, stress out, and never do it. Instead, write something like "create a book title" or "write a single paragraph".

A great example of this in nature is how a beaver builds its dam. The beaver starts with a small twig, and then builds on top of that by adding more and more twigs until the dam is complete. By starting small and then adding on, the beaver is able to create a sturdy structure that will last.

By being specific with your to-do list items, you are setting yourself up for success and ensuring that you will actually get things done. This approach alone will make you 100x more productive.

DON'T BREAK THE CHAIN

I know this may be scary for some of you, as it seems like a commitment. But remember, the chart is just a silly drawing. What you put in it can vary. Accept that not all days will be incredibly productive. However, fill it out with something, anything at all, and you will be better off than you were. One step closer to your goal and well-being is better than none.

If you write one paragraph a day, roughly 200 words, in a year's time you'll have written 73,000 words. Enough for a book. Small actions over a long time can pay off big and have have ripple effects into the rest of your life.

> *"As it is not one swallow or a fine day that makes a spring, so it is not one day or a short time that makes a man blessed and happy."*
> — ARISTOTLE

Jerry Seinfeld is considered one of the top comedians of all time. He is also the co-creator and co-writer of Seinfeld, a sitcom has claimed countless awards, and is largely considered one of the more successful tv series. Seinfeld reached his peak in earnings in 1998, when he reportedly earned $267 million dollars.[73] The TV show which first aired in 1989 is still airing in 2022.

But it's not just the accolades or earnings that are fascinating about Jerry Seinfeld. It's his consistency of producing high quality content and entertainment.

Brad Isaac was a young comedian just starting out, when he met Jerry Seinfeld backstage. According to an interview with LifeHacker, this is how their interaction unfolded after he asked if he had any tips for a young comic:

He said the way to be a better comic was to create better jokes and the way to create better jokes was to write every day.

He told me to get a big wall calendar that has a whole year on one page and hang it on a prominent wall. The next step was to get a big red magic marker. He said for each day that I do my task of writing, I get to put a big red X over that day.

"After a few days you'll have a chain. Just keep at it and the chain will grow longer every day. You'll like seeing that chain, especially when you get a few weeks under your belt. Your only job is to not break the chain."[74]

Stay consistent and it'll become a habit. And if you do skip a day for whatever reason, pick it up the next day. It's important that you don't allow yourself to come up with reasons not to do it. Don't think of the chart as a chore; rather view it as a daily insight into yourself and a tool to make you happier.

THE ZEIGARNIK EFFECT

At the end of the day, *erase your board* and start the next day start with a clean slate. Don't leave incomplete tasks on the board to pile up. That can have a negative psychological effect. It is known as the Zeigarnik effect, where we tend to remember incomplete or interrupted tasks more easily than complete ones. Sometimes the effect is useful; this can be used to our advantage when studying, for example, where taking breaks to do unrelated tasks can help us remember things better.

However, for productivity purposes, this can contribute to stress. Remember, even if you did 1/10 tasks that you wrote, you are still moving forward. Seeing uncompleted tasks may be discouraging and make you less likely to do them tomorrow. Instead, erase your board, and the next day add the task back if it's still needed. If the task was too difficult, try to break it down further into smaller tasks, or slightly modify it. Instead of calling a client for a sales pitch, try contacting a client and simply introducing yourself and asking how they are. Instead of meal planning your whole week, plan the meal for tomorrow.

THE ELEPHANT IN THE ROOM

It's easy to start with very small tasks and to put things on your board that you'd do anyway. But over time you should start slowly adding things that you may be a little uncomfortable with. Then, work your way up to doing things that may even scare you. It could be emailing your resume to a company you otherwise wouldn't approach. Expressing your feelings to someone you like. Or maybe for you it's to skydive in the desert. When you do unexpected things, you'll find that you also get unexpected results. The whole point of The Method is to learn, grow, and move forward. So it's important to start challenging yourself and not become stagnant.

Telling you to get out of your comfort zone is very cliché. You've heard it before and it hurts to write it. So I'll say it in another way, so you can have a new perspective on the phrase.

Every single thing you love right now is a result of you taking a leap of faith at some point. Your friends, your favorite meal, your current job, the person you're dating, your hobbies— everything. You had to take a risk to get any of those things. And it wasn't always easy. You had to put yourself out there. You had to try something new. You had to be vulnerable. And it was scary. But you did it anyway. And now, here you are. You've made it through all of those scary moments, and you're better for it.

It's funny that they call it the comfort zone. It sounds pleasant. Like a place we should all strive to be in. So why do they keep telling us to get out of it? The truth is, your comfort zone is your prison. It's a cell with padded walls and a comfy bed. It's a place where you feel safe, but it's also a place where you're not growing. You're not learning. You're not challenged. You're not living.

THE METHOD

There's a horrible practice that circuses use to keep the elephants in place. They tie the front leg of a baby elephant to a stake in the ground using a chain. The baby elephant will pull this chain but quickly realize they are unable to break out. It doesn't take long for them to reach their behemoth size. But here's the thing: for most elephants, that same chain will hold them in place, despite that it can now easily break out of it. People are always asking why doesn't the elephant do it? A better question is why don't you? How many of these invisible chains are holding you back?

Someone once said, "If you want something you've never had you must be willing to do something you've never done." You have to be willing to risk your comfort for a chance at happiness. We need to take risks in life to discover new things that we may end up loving. All of us have extraordinary potential, but whether we reach it is a choice, not destiny.

CONCLUSION:

Just start. Wherever you are, whatever you want to achieve - just start. There's no better time than right now.

CHAPTER SEVEN

BOOST YOUR PRODUCTIVITY

There are some excellent tricks when it comes to being productive and effective:

THE PERILS OF A RUDDERLESS SHIP

Doc Rivers, a coach of the Boston Celtics basketball team, is considered one of the best in the world. While with the Celtics in 2008, he was haunted by pressure of coaching one of the most historically successful franchises in the NBA. But the team hadn't won since 1986. That year's roster included all-star players - Ray Allen, Kevin Garnett, and Paul Pierce. With 16 winning banners hanging in their arena every time they stepped in, the pressure couldn't be greater for Doc Rivers that season.

Doc Rivers described those banners as "...staring at you every day, like you are not worth it. That's how I felt. Like every day you walk into the arena, 'We haven't done that.'" One night, Rivers was thinking of how to get his team focused and give them some pressure as well. He remembered that the JFK and Martin Luther King's burial site had a flame that never goes out. He couldn't do that, so instead he came up with a light. And he asked for a light to be installed and shined at the empty spot in the Celtics facility where the 17th championship banner would go.

After the next practice, he explained to the players that this light would never go off as long as they don't win the championship. It was to be the only focus they were to have and play for. They saw the light every day in every practice. The Celtics ended up winning the championship in 2008 and that was the only championship they won since. It's important to have clear-cut goals and know why you're doing what you're doing. Without having a goal, it is pointless to devise steps to get there.

Earl Nightingale once said, "Think of a ship with the complete voyage mapped out and planned. The captain and crew know exactly where the ship is going and how long it will take — it has a definite goal. And 9,999 times out of 10,000, it will get there. Now let's take another ship — just like the first — only let's not put a crew on it, or a captain at the helm. Let's give it no aiming point, no goal, and no destination. We just start the engines and let it go. I think you'll agree that if it gets out of the harbor at all, it will either sink or wind up on some deserted beach — a derelict. It can't go anyplace because it has no destination and no guidance."

WRITE IT DOWN

The world-renowned Richard Branson, founder of the expansive Virgin Group with 400 companies, has a net worth of $4.8 billion. But one of his essential tools is surprisingly humble - a notebook. Branson advocates for writing down ideas, no matter how small, as the best way to ensure that those thoughts don't vanish overnight. "But don't just take notes for the sake of taking notes, go through your ideas and turn them into actionable and measurable goals," he advises [72]. Taking notes is more than just a habit; it helps to declutter the mind, store ideas and turn them into reality. It's a simple but effective tool for highly efficient people - like Richard Branson.

A notebook can also serve more than just a productivity tool. It's a great place to express your feelings and to write down anything else that's weighing in your thoughts. So, if you're looking to get that next big idea off the ground, or to simply declutter your mind, try taking a page out of Richard Branson's book and invest in a notebook.

SCHEDULE YOUR TIME IN MINUTES, NOT HOURS

The Method will help you balance your life, but you can make it even more effective by supplementing it with other tools. Start simple. But over time, I highly recommend keeping a calendar with 15-minute intervals in addition to completing your daily chart. It will help you to maximize your time, and you'll be surprised at what you can fit into small time windows. Marissa Meyer, the Yahoo CEO, conducts some meetings with colleagues in as little as 5 minutes![33] Most successful people schedule things in minutes, not hours.[34] You should invest the first part of your day working on something that will have the most significant impact on reaching your goal. You should also prioritize the most essential things in your life first. Once you get comfortable with the idea of The Method and keeping a calendar, you can start scheduling everything. You'll find that scheduling something will save you a ton of time. Instead of constantly checking your emails, social media, you can do it several times a day during the time you have scheduled. There are many tools that you can use to make The Method more effective. However, keep The Method at the core. It's easy to start neglecting things that hold you together and tip yourself off balance again.

THE MOST UNDERUSED PRODUCTIVITY TOOL

Our most powerful money- and time-saving tool is vastly underutilized: our imaginations. We often imagine our future and our days, but rarely do we use it as a tool to increase productivity. We all tend to get ideas, but seldom do we see them through, using only our imaginations. We often rush to meetings, to writing, or to paying for things to see if they will work. However, there may be another way.

Perhaps you've heard of an engineer named Nikola Tesla, the man responsible for many technologies that have revolutionized the world. He designed the alternating-current (AC) system; he earned over 700 different patents. In his autobiography, Tesla described his own method behind these revolutionary inventions:

"My method is different. I do not rush into actual work. When I get an idea, I start at once building it up in my imagination. I change the construction, make improvements and operate the device in my mind. It is absolutely immaterial to me whether I run my turbine in thought or test it in my shop. I even note if it is out of balance. There is no difference whatever, the results are the same. In this way, I am able to rapidly develop and perfect a conception without touching anything. When I have gone so far as to embody in the invention every possible improvement I can think of and see no fault anywhere, I put into concrete form this final product of my brain. Invariably my device works as I conceived that it should, and the experiment comes out exactly as I planned it. In twenty years there has not been a single exception. Why should it be otherwise? Engineering, electrical, and mechanical, is positive in results. There is scarcely a subject that cannot be mathematically treated, and the effects calculated or the results determined beforehand from the available theoretical and practical data. The carrying out into practice of a crude idea as is being generally done is, I hold, nothing but a waste of energy, money and time." [32]

Drawing on his extraordinary grasp of physics and engineering, he was able to plan, construct and test revolutionary inventions right in his head. While this requires an exceptional level of intelligence and creativity, we can all benefit from using our imaginations more. By doing so, we can avoid wasting time in unnecessary meetings, testing and editing - and get straight to the heart of the problem. With practice, we can even complete projects entirely in our heads, only having to make them real afterwards. So next time you're faced with a problem, take a few moments to imagine different solutions and work them out in your head. It could save you time and energy, and might even lead to unexpected breakthroughs.

ONE AND DONE RULE

No, it's not a reference to college basketball. It's a technique that many successful leaders employ. Have you ever received a parking ticket in the mail, read it, but decided to deal with it later? Or read an e-mail and closed it, intending to respond later? Effective people don't do that. If it's a task that consumes less than 10 minutes, they deal with it right away. This way, you are not wasting your time twice on the same task. It reduces stress. It also reduces problems that may come up if those tasks are forgotten or late. One and done.

KOBE'S KNEES

Successful people know the importance of work. They also know the importance of putting it down once it's time to go home. You'll learn about the importance of balance throughout this book. Balance means working when it's work time—and disconnecting when it's not. Setting clear boundaries with your employer. This is even more important if the employer is yourself. As a self-employed professional, found I was a horrible boss to myself. Working on weekends, sacrificing valuable time with others to answer emails, and working for very little pay.

Once we let the boundaries blur, everything suffers. Successful people plan out their day minute by minute. They don't waste time, and thus, they always make it home for dinner –and can enjoy that dinner without checking their email in the middle. Use The Method as a guide to be efficient, and you'll get weeks' worth of work done in hours. You'll learn how to work smarter, not harder.

Tim Grover was the trainer of the greatest basketball player of all time, Michael Jordan. He talked about the excruciating work ethic of one of the best athletes of our time. However, what made MJ so successful was not working hard. It was working smart. He surrounded himself with the right team. Grover reveals that he would watch MJ's last game's tape and count by hand how many steps he took with each leg. He would do this to know which of his legs requires more attention or rest. Without this crucial efficiency, working out harder could lead to injuries and be detrimental to a player's condition. Another basketball great known for his maniacal work ethic, Kobe Bryant, complained to MJ that his knees were killing him. Jordan knew just who to recommend.

Before Grover, Bryant had a heap of personnel, including a massage therapist, doctor, and team trainer. All of them had their own plan. Grover's very first step was to get everybody on the same page. After analyzing everything, Grover concluded that at age 30, Kobe was working too much. "Athleticism implies two things – acceleration and deceleration. Kobe was overworking his acceleration ability (concentric contractions), which shortens the muscles, and neglecting his deceleration ability (eccentric contractions), which lengthen the muscles. Because of that, every time he would land, change direction, etc. the muscles couldn't take the load, so the cartilage and bones did. Thirteen years of that left its toll," said Grover.[76]

His solution? To completely take out the concentric phase of training. He had to come up with a creative approach. He would have his team lift up Kobe's weights, to only have Kobe do the negative motion. This would elongate his muscles and take the pressure off his knees. It worked. In the next two years, Bryant would lead his team to victory in NBA finals and win two MVP awards. Ultimately, doing less resulted in achieving more and probably saving Kobe Bryant's career in the process.

CONCLUSION:

Write it all down. It reduces stress and helps you plan. Effective people complete any task that's less than 10 minutes in one go. Work smarter, not harder.

CHAPTER EIGHT

WHAT THE WORLD'S SMARTEST PEOPLE KNOW

I mentioned that other self-improvement methods will undoubtedly fail you because they are not tailored to you, and they lack crucial ingredients. It can take years of trying and failing to learn key life lessons. But what if you could take a shortcut and learn some of the most critical lessons from the world's smartest and most successful people now? Just being aware of these can improve your chances of achieving your goals.

Life can fly by in the blink of an eye, leaving us unaware of the possibilities that are within our reach. In this book, I offer proven, practical strategies that are simple to implement and can have a remarkable impact on your life. If you take the time to learn and apply the principles I share, you will discover that life can be easier, more enjoyable, and far more rewarding.

You may have already come across some of these. There is a good reason for this, but I hope these stories will give you a different perspective and another reason to incorporate them into your life.

THE HAPPINESS PARADOX

The word "happy" and "happiness" seem to be everywhere these days - including this book. Everyone is always trying to tell us how to be happy or how to reach it. But the truth is, happiness isn't something you can climb to or a destination you reach. It's an emotion, and at best, a temporary state of being. Would it even be possible to feel happy without the lows of sadness, fear, and anger? Wouldn't we just be? Our level of happiness is constantly shifting - minute by minute and day by day.

Questions like "Are we happy in our relationship?", "Are we happy with our job?" and "Are we happy about our kid?" can't be answered properly, as they don't take into account the ever-changing nature of happiness. The fairer way to ask these questions would be to phrase them with the words "right now" or "generally".

If we strive for happiness as an end goal, we will only find ourselves more miserable. We should view it as one of many pitstops along our journey. We should make every effort to make this pitstop more accessible and easier to reach. Hopefully, something you take away from this book will help you do just that.

There's a Taoist parable called Sai Weng Shi Ma, that's about a poor Chinese farmer which goes like this:

A long time ago, a poor Chinese farmer lost a horse. When his neighbors heard the news, they said, "Well that's too bad." The farmer simply replied, "Maybe." But then, the horse returned with another one in tow. The neighbors said, "Well that's good fortune." The farmer again said, "Maybe." The next day, the farmer's son attempted to tame the new horse, but he fell and broke his leg. All the neighbors said, "Well that's too bad." The farmer replied again, "Maybe." Shortly after, the emperor declared war on a neighboring nation and ordered all able-bodied men to come fight. Many were killed or badly maimed, but the farmer's son was spared due to his injury. The neighbors said, "Well that's good fortune." The farmer said, "Maybe." And so the story goes. [77]

It's often that our biggest misfortunes lead to our greatest moments. Until the day our lives come to an end, we will never know which things in our life will bring us the most joy. Therefore, the next time you experience a setback, and someone tells you how bad it is, why not just take a deep breath and think to yourself, "Maybe."

WHY NASA USES A COUNTDOWN FOR LAUNCHING SPACE SHUTTLES

Patience is a quickly disappearing quality in our society. It's the byproduct of new technologies that provide instant gratification and perform tasks quicker than ever. It's perhaps also due to the glorification of the modern entrepreneurial mindset. But moving too quickly comes at a cost.

Impatience can lead to mistakes and missed opportunities, ruin your credibility, and make you look desperate. Be too pushy, and a buyer may walk away. Reply too quickly, and it may make you look desperate. Rush a project, and a small missed detail may burn it to the ground.

A good example of this is when Nike let one of the best basketball players on the planet slip through its fingers. When Stephen Curry entered the NBA, he signed an endorsement deal with Nike. This wasn't uncommon as two thirds of all NBA players signed with the brand. However, in 2013 his contract was up for renewal. During their meeting, according to Stephen Curry's father, Dell, Nike executives mispronounced his name and never bothered to correct it. But that wasn't the worst of it. During a PowerPoint slide, one of the slides accidentally featured another player's name, presumably left over from repurposed materials. Dell says he stopped paying attention to the presentation after that. Nike's people had rushed the presentation, and their carelessness showed as a lack of concern. It was no surprise that Stephen Curry signed with another brand, Under Armour. This simple rushed presentation resulted in skyrocketing the popularity of Under Armour and the loss of millions of dollars in revenue for Nike.

While impatience can lead to problems, being patient has surprising benefits. It can make you be perceived as more attractive, your business more lucrative, and in higher demand. Not to mention, it may prevent you from making bad decisions.

Even after years of meticulously planning a launch, NASA uses a countdown for launching their space shuttles. This routine does more than build anticipation and create excitement. It allows technicians and astronauts to synchronize their moves, go through the checklists, and make any last-minute adjustments. In 1994, a space shuttle called Endeavor aborted its takeoff with just 1.9 seconds left on the countdown to liftoff. It took nearly 300,000 gallons of water to hose the shuttle down. The shuttle was building up to its maximum takeoff power when sensors detected excessive heat in the fuel pump and computers shut down the system automatically. All the astronauts were able to get out safely, because NASA took its time. While our lives typically don't involve billion-dollar space ships, there are many times where we could use a countdown ourselves to prevent us from sending an e-mail too early or making a hasty business decision.

One practical way to apply this would be when sending e-mails or messages. If the message is somewhat important, type it out and let a little time pass before sending it out. If a decision or e-mail is really significant, sleep on it. Take that anxious and trigger-happy time to ask questions. Think about what questions you haven't thought of asking yet. Once you start asking yourself the hard questions, details will start appearing that may influence how you respond. You can also use this time to consider the perspective of the person on the receiving end. This will help you be not only more empathetic but to maximize the outcome of the situation. So whether you want to finalize a deal or make weekend plans, considering the perspective of the other person will bring you closer to your end goal.

Gmail has a neat feature that allows you to delay sending your e-mail by 5, 10, 20, or 30 seconds. I can't tell you how many times this has saved me not only from grammatical errors but poor decisions. There's something about that moment of clarity immediately after you make a bad decision.

And sometimes, being patient and taking your time to respond can actually strengthen your position. Take the unusual example of a prank orchestrated by a journalist named Oobah Butler, who managed to turn his backyard shed into the top-rated restaurant in London on TripAdvisor. He used ridiculous but surprisingly effective techniques to pull it off. He used an array of fake reviews from friends. He photographed plates of food created using inedible household products such as shaving cream and dishwasher tablets to make them artier. He also made the restaurant reservation-only. But what skyrocketed the restaurant's popularity was Butler declining all the requests for reservations. According to Butler, this drove people mad and they wanted to get in even more. He was flooded with calls and messages. TV execs even used their work e-mails in an attempt to secure a reservation at this exclusive restaurant. While all of this was just a prank, it's a great demonstration of how patience, or unavailability, in this case, can increase your perceived value.

If you think this is a fluke, how many times have you walked past a restaurant with a long line and thought to yourself that it must be pretty good, just because people are waiting for it? The tech giant, Apple, doesn't just throw their new products into the store; they build anticipation. Strategically apply the same principles to our availability and decision-making. It will make other people value your time.

There's power in being patient. I experienced this myself when I was selling a domain name many years ago. I posted it for sale in online forums with a "make an offer" option. I went on a trip and forgot all about it. A month later, I checked my account and it was filled with messages from the same person. I opened the first message and they asked if I would take $500 for the name. If I'd seen the offer, I would've immediately accepted it as I'd paid only $15 for it. But I wasn't there to read the message. Several days later, the same buyer sent a message offering $1,000. I would've been ecstatic at this point and would've jumped on the offer. But I still wasn't there. In their last message, the buyer seemed to get even more desperate and their offer jumped to $1,500! All of this happened without a single reply or negotiation from me. The buyer must've assumed their offer wasn't significant enough to even get a response from me, so because of their impatience, they raised their price and negotiated against themselves. In the end, they overpaid for a mediocre name and I made a lot more money than I expected. Sometimes a buyer will walk away if you say "no" too many times or ignore them for too long. But just as likely, a buyer may walk away if you jump on their offer too quickly. They may question their decision. Did they offer too much? Is the seller desperate?

Applying the same principles in social situations can also pay dividends, especially if you're very interested in another person. Overwhelm them with quick replies and long messages too early, and you will be seen as desperate and needy. Do the opposite and they may perceive you as more valuable. It makes sense because their insecurities play into the equation.

Additionally, someone who seems busy appears that they have more things going on in their life. This makes them more attractive. We all want things that we can't have or are hard to obtain. If someone is throwing themselves at you, their perceived value goes down.

The rush of spontaneity can be exciting and a quick decision may alleviate anxiety. But once it fades, you are left with the poor decisions that you made. Oftentimes, there is no road back either. I encourage you to live spontaneously, but also realize that sometimes it's best to let things unfold on their own. Sometimes patience is productive procrastination. Sometimes it's allowing the seed you planted to grow. Sometimes it's letting go of the wheel and realizing you are only a passenger.

As Jean-Jacques Rousseau once said, "Patience is bitter, but its fruit is sweet".

Notice the next time you have to wait for something; a video to load longer than a few seconds, a longer article, a bit of traffic. Do the few seconds make you frustrated? Raise your blood pressure? It's not time that's escaping us in those moments. It's our self-control, happiness, and health.

THE BENEFITS OF BEING AN OUTCAST

Most of us share a common struggle that comes to define us for most of our childhood, teens, and even well into our adulthood. Driven by our need to feel accepted and be loved, we want to fit in, whether it's with our nose-picking kindergarten friends or colleagues in Wall Street who end up using the nose for something else entirely. We're constantly being told to just be ourselves, but few practice what they preach, and we often punish others – and ourselves – for doing so. This struggle between being ourselves and fitting in is one that many of us are unable to escape.

There's a big debate in the psychological community of how much of a role nature versus nurture plays in our personalities. Is it our genetics that determine who we become, or our environment? Is it both? If so, what percentage is one or the other? Ultimately, I think it's very clear that our environment, albeit not the only factor, plays a huge role in our development. Thus, we start with a clean slate (or as much as our genetics allow) and develop unique personalities, quirks, and ambitions. But as we progress through life, all these things get diluted, if not lost altogether. With every new social circle we enter, we lose a bit of ourselves. This is true especially in our younger years, as we are extremely sensitive to criticism and what others think of us. This fear is what drives us to mask more and more of ourselves in a bid to fit in.

Unfortunately, the cost of fitting in is diminishing what is unique and interesting about you. We're willing to sacrifice that to gain acceptance and avoid backlash. What's funny is that later on in life, the very few things that we have left unique about ourselves are what set us apart. Those quirks that we tried to hide in our youth are the very same things that people love and become attracted to. If you're in the drama club in high school, you may be considered weird or an outcast. But tell people you're an actor later on in life and they'll brag about you to all their friends. You may be ridiculed for your strange hair in your early years, only to grow up and get compliments for the same wacky curls. Why is this? It's partly because we're more mature and our interests may change, but I think it's simpler than that. It's because once we all go through the phase of fitting in for everyone, so many people and things are the same that we are gasping to find something that stands out and speaks to us.

Conformity is boring. We secretly want to connect to those small unique pieces that we lost or hid.

A quote from Friedrich Nietzsche stuck with me. It was simple but powerful. It said, "Become who you are." This clicked for me because I interpreted it as embracing and fighting to bring out your authentic self. Not wasting your time living as someone else. One of the reasons we always fall short of our expectations is because we strive to imitate someone else, only to realize that we can really only be ourselves.

To become who we are, we have to carve our own path. If the pioneers in history taught us anything, it's that the best innovations and inventions don't come from following blueprints. No great idea comes without skepticism or ridicule either.

In the early part of the 1900s, rumors spread that two brothers, Wilbur and Orville Wright, were working on a flying machine. Although there had been some attempts to bring airplanes to the sky, these experiments were highly ridiculed by the public and media. But growing up in a family that encouraged the pursuit of knowledge and hard work, the brothers didn't give up. Over the next few years, they would research flying, test theories, and develop flight control and propulsion systems. In 1903, against all odds, they would be the first in the world to make a powered, sustained, and controlled flight. The Wright brothers are now known as the pioneers of aviation. They paved the path for modern-day travel.

Think of the knowledge that you gain from your parents, school, and work as Lego pieces. The more pieces you acquire, the more different things you can build. The pieces don't dictate exactly what, how, and how quickly to build. They are not instructions. They are simply building blocks. So discard, rearrange, rebuild, and create a brilliant masterpiece that is yours.

It's not always easy to be or do something unique. After all, even today, you share the earth with billions of people. Billions more came before that. Kirby Ferguson, a Canadian filmmaker, says that, "everything is a remix." Everything comes from something else. Every thought that you will ever have comes from something else. Creativity is mostly a combination of three elements – copy, transform and combine. Someone once said, "good artists copy, great artists steal."

That doesn't mean that you should just borrow wholesale from others; you've probably also heard the saying "don't reinvent the wheel." (Although ironically, the wheel has been reinvented repeatedly over thousands of years.) What started as a round, irregular wooden construct in 3200 BC has evolved into modern tires engineered with manmade materials with unbelievable precision, that allow us to travel safely at previously inconceivable speeds.

So be lawless. Surprise yourself. Don't give up on the things that make you weird, as these are the very things that will prove to be the most interesting about you. Create things that may shock people or even make them laugh. Don't worry about fitting in, or fret about trying to come up with something entirely unique. Use advice, knowledge, and the lives of others as tools to carve your path rather than a compass.

REMEMBER THE PYRAMID

Psychologist Abraham Maslow theorized that human behavior can be broken down into responding to five basic needs, visualized in the form of a pyramid. At the base of the pyramid are our physiological needs, such as air, water, and food. As we move up the pyramid, our needs become increasingly abstract, including the need for love and belonging, esteem, and ultimately, self-actualization. The takeaway is not the categories themselves but how we prioritize and function in order to fulfill our needs.

It is essential to take care of the basics before we work on anything else. If we don't have air to breathe or food to eat, everything else at the top of the pyramid will become irrelevant almost immediately. Only after we take care of these necessary needs can we start being productive and happy. Although most of us are not gasping for air or suffering from water shortages, we need to begin considering other things that prevent us from being the best we can be each day. We must devote time to address those underlying issues. Even if we devote a small amount of time toward addressing our problems every day, we will feel a lot better.

We tend to overlook fundamental things such as love or our health and focus on the top of the pyramid, only for everything to come crashing down when our health declines or our relationships fail. Therefore, keep this little pyramid in mind when deciding what to add to your list of daily activities.

WHY BUDDHIST MONKS GIVE UP THEIR POSSESSIONS

When Buddhist monks come into the monastic life, the first thing they do is give up their possessions. They believe that when you have fewer things to care for and be responsible for, you have more time to work on yourself. It frees up your mind. Monks shave their heads and are given only two sets of clothes. Just by having hair, you already have a multitude of issues that you have to deal with every day. You have to consider your choice of hair products, barber, stylist, current trends, people's opinions, the current state of your hair, etc. Just by having hair, you already have 10 more problems than a Buddhist monk does. Next, think about your wardrobe. You have dozens of different outfits and shoes for every occasion. All your clothes have to be washed, stored, matched, and taken care of. Buddhists wear their clothing only for its intended purpose, not fashion. Because they have fewer things, they have fewer problems to deal with. It isn't just monks that realized this. Barrack Obama, the former president of United States, wore only gray or blue suits. When asked about it, he said "I'm trying to pare down decisions. I don't want to make decisions about what I'm eating or wearing. Because I have too many other decisions to make." [71] Each of the things that you have in your life takes up more than physical space. It occupies space in your mind as well. Each of the things that you own comes with separate problems and responsibilities. I'm not suggesting you shave your head, throw out all your clothing, or sell your car. But what you can do is find the middle ground. Find the excess occupying space in your mind and life and reduce it.

SEIZE OPPORTUNITIES

The goal of The Method is not only to balance your life but to also open up doors that weren't open for you before. Once you start to actively move towards your goals, no matter how slowly, you'll find yourself getting new opportunities. From an outside perspective, it may seem like these opportunities come with flashing lights, but you may not notice them. Sometimes people will stick to The Method a little too strictly, and instead of decluttering and getting more free time, they'll feel like they are busy. After all, you filled up all the categories with tasks, right? How can you have time for anything else?

However, the goal is a *balanced life.* When a good opportunity presents itself, you should jump on it and ditch some of the things you may have planned. Remember, your list gets wiped clean every day; nothing there should prevent you from taking advantage of an unexpected opportunity. Good opportunities don't come knocking twice. If you get that big audition, an invitation to an amazing trip, find that other person you've been looking for – jump on it! After all, these opportunities are what we work for.

But be selective. Some things may be disguised as opportunities or cool events. But you'll find they are simply draining your time and throwing everything off balance. Not every party needs your attendance. Not every business opportunity is a good one. Don't forget to take risks, but value your time. Over time, you'll develop a sense of when it's smart to stick to your list, and when it's time to take a chance.

HAVE THREE HANDS

You may wonder how successful people get to where they are with such limited time every day. The simple secret, as we've seen, is efficiency. But the secret to efficiency is outsourcing. Successful people are great at utilizing resources. They build networks and outsource some of their days. You can look at this as cheating or taking shortcuts. But it's a crucial part of making your life easier and more successful. Take a movie for example. One person could technically write the script, direct it, act in it, and produce the movie. Yet, more than likely, they won't. It makes more sense to pay for someone to do a bit of the work or to utilize your friends. But you don't have to be a movie director to outsource work.

An Italian economist and philosopher by the name of Vilfredo Pareto noticed 20% of the pea plants in his garden produced 80% of the healthy pea pods. This caused him to take a look at uneven distribution in other walks of life. He discovered that 80% of land in Italy was owned by 20% of the population. That 80% of the production came from just 20% of the companies. He came to the conclusion that 80% of the results will come from 20% of your actions.[35] In business, it is now known as the 80/20 rule. If you examine your daily routine, you'll likely find the same results. You'll find that not only this is true in your business, it is probably true in your personal life.

For example, maybe 20% of your wardrobe is worn 80% of the time. Thus, you could organize your wardrobe to make it more accessible. Or you could even donate most of your other clothes without affecting your style. As a business, you may notice that 80% of your sales are due to 20% of your product. Hence, you may want to focus on that 20%. In healthcare, 80% of the budget is spent on 20% of the population.[36] There's a ton of inefficiency in our lives, which if fixed, can free up a lot of time and money.

Everyday tasks like doing the laundry, responding to emails, updating social media and other mundane tasks take up most of your time. They use most of your effort points. Imagine if those tasks were out of your way. How much time and stress would that save?

The downside to outsourcing is that you lose some of the control and thus the quality may suffer. Depending on what you are outsourcing, your credibility may suffer as well. Once, a critical infrastructure company hired a risk team to investigate abnormalities in their logs. After a security check, the team found unusual activity and daily logins from China. Fearing hackers, the team performed an in-depth investigation. The investigation took a funky turn when instead of a hacker, the connections were traced back to an employee described as a quiet family man in his forties, whom you would not give a second look. He was also the company's top-performing programmer.

The logs indicated that daily connections from Shenyang, China were coming in using this employee's credentials, spanning the entire workday. It was strange because a physical token was needed in order to access the system. Yet, the employee was in his office, day after day, diligently working at his desk in his US office. After checking his computer and desk, the team found hundreds of invoices. Invoices made out to third-party developers based in – you guessed it – Shenyang, China. Turns out, this employee had discovered an ingenious way to lighten his workload. He would pass on his programming work to a team in China, and then pass it back to management in his company.

Was it effective? Well, he was able to earn a six-figure salary and outsource it for one-fifth of the price. He received praise several years in a row for his code. Apparently, it was "clean, well-written, submitted in a timely fashion." He was routinely named the best developer in the building. After checking his web browsing history, the company found that he didn't just "lighten" his workload. A normal schedule for him looked something like this:

9:00 AM - arrival, surfing on Reddit and watching cat videos

11:30 AM - lunch

1:00 PM - shopping on eBay

2:00 PM - Facebook and LinkedIn

4:40 PM - progress report to management

5 PM - going home.

This method worked so well for him that he took on work at several other companies and did the same thing.[37] Needless to say, after his secret was discovered, he no longer works at the original company.

Work isn't the only thing being outsourced. With an incredible rise of dating apps and the majority of connections occurring online, many find themselves too busy or not experienced enough to find dates. That's where online dating managers come in. There's an influx of websites offering to manage your dating life for you. Sounds too good to be true? Tim Ferris, author of "The 4-Hour Workweek," disagrees. A big advocate for outsourcing, Ferris decided to experiment in outsourcing his dating. He hired 4-5 teams scattered around the world to find women and set up coffee dates. To prevent a logistical nightmare, he booked his dates in back-to-back 20 minute "sessions" in 3 different cafes on the same exact street. His experiment ended up being so successful that he wound up on 20 dates, meeting a long-term girlfriend in the process.[38]

Another downside to outsourcing is that you are also not gaining experience. Experience that you would otherwise get if you were to do these tasks yourself and figure things out. So, it's important to find a good balance between outsourcing and doing things on your own. Try to handle things yourself; if you find yourself at a point where the task is taking too much time, then employ some help. There was one instance where I had trouble with one of my websites. I tried to fix it, but at my speed, it would have taken me another day or two to figure it out. So I hired a web developer, and he fixed it in twenty minutes for $25. We often don't want to pay anyone else for something we can do ourselves, but we have to ask ourselves, is this really worth our time? If someone said to you, I will pay you $25 to work for two days, would you? Could you make more money doing something else with your time? Money aside, time is our most precious commodity and it shouldn't be wasted. (Even this book is partly outsourced! – I used an editor to go over the text, which most authors do.)

Focus on tasks that are responsible for most of your desired results. Hire a personal assistant for the others. Find a way to automate whatever tasks you can. Stop micromanaging and striving for perfection. Learn to let go of the reins, and outsource to maximize your time and effort.

HOW TO STRESS LESS AND HAVE MORE MEANINGFUL INTERACTIONS

Even with our highly digital society, relationships will affect nearly everything in your life. To get ahead you still need to know how to deal with people effectively. This part could be a whole book by itself. (I highly recommend reading "How to Win Friends and Influence People" by Dale Carnegie, which is a great handbook in basic psychology on how to deal with people.) There's plenty to learn about human interaction, but there are some simple ways to improve every single interaction and your chances in getting what you want. I know this sounds like manipulation. That's the impression that I got when I started reading Dale Carnegie's book. But in reality, these "tricks" are nothing more than things that we should all practice when dealing with people. They can actually help us to be better and kinder human beings.

A simple realization that came to me a few years ago changed the way I view people. Most of us tend to lose patience with those who are less than intelligent, share different views, or otherwise fall short of our expectations. A conversation, sale, or entire relationship can crumble as a result of this. What changed for me is changing the way I perceive intelligence.

What I came to understand is that we perceive intelligence incorrectly. Each one of us has a limited amount of effort points. Each day, we can perform a limited amount of activities. Money, time, weather, health, stamina, focus, and other factors limit us. So each of us (if we have that luxury) can choose where to spend those effort points each day. Some people may not be fortunate enough to attend universities or school. While you might spend your effort points on education, others may spend theirs on other skills, expanding areas of intelligence other than linguistic or logical-mathematical.

A farmer may not be able to converse about abstract expressionism, but they will have a keen understanding of agriculture and have specific technical skills like operating a tractor. (And if you think that's easy, you've never sat in the cab of a tractor.) Einstein may have been able to teach you about the Theory of Relativity but lack the social skills to approach a woman. A bodybuilder at the gym may not be the greatest conversationalist in general topics, but when it comes to nutrition or kinesiology, they may have expert knowledge and understanding.

> *"Everyone is a genius. But if you judge a fish by its ability to climb a tree, it will live its whole life believing that it is stupid."*
>
> -UNKNOWN

Intelligence can be found in the most unexpected places. Let's take Joe Exotic, the zookeeper featured on the hit documentary, Tiger King. After watching the show, you may conclude that he is less intelligent than your average man, to put it kindly. Yet, when it comes to naturalistic intelligence, he is far smarter than an average person. He has a much better understanding animal behavior than most. As you begin to examine people in this broader concept of intelligence, you will begin to see that most are pretty smart in some way. We just spent our effort points in different ways. This simple realization has improved every single interaction that I had since. But I encourage you to delve even deeper.

We judge intelligence by the wrong criteria. School testing only measures these book-smart abilities: test-taking, memorization, following directions, reading, problem-solving, and logic. But there is much more to intelligence, and many different kinds. According to developmental psychologist Howard Gardner, there are actually 9 types of intelligence:

-**Bodily-kinesthetic** – coordinating your mind with your body.

-**Interpersonal** – sensing people's feelings and motives.

-**Existential** – tackling the questions of why we live, and why we die.

-**Logical-mathematical** – quantifying things, making hypotheses, and proving them.

-**Musical** – discerning sounds, their pitch, tone, rhythm, and timbre.

-**Naturalist** – understanding living things and reading nature.

-**Spatial** – visualizing the world in 3D.

-**Intra-personal** – understanding yourself, what you feel, and what you want.

-**Linguistic** – finding the right words to express and what you mean.

THE METHOD

How many of these do we test for in a school or anywhere else? What about other things that could be interpreted as types of intelligence? Think about charisma, humor, or street-smarts. Without evaluating all these, we cannot determine someone's true intelligence.

The type of environment plays a huge role. Let's take someone incredibly gifted when it comes to book-smarts, like Einstein. Let's throw him into a theater performance, basketball game, or a dating show. How would one of the world's smartest men fare then? You may be smart in your own element, but step out of your comfort zone, and you may find yourself to be the dummy. Even in the same intelligence category, your perceived intelligence isn't an absolute measure. Take the world's best English professor and let him try to teach Chinese. Take a sprinter and put him into a long-distance race. They may adapt more quickly than you or I, they may fare better than a person of another type of intelligence, but when it comes to an outsider's eye – they are just another dummy. Next time you judge someone, think about how you'd look if they took you out of your element. And if you are always the smartest person in the room, it's time to switch rooms.

To fully understand someone, we also have to take a glimpse at their past environments. After all, we are a product of our environment. It helps us understand people's behavior and where their opinions come from. It's not race, gender, or age that determines the way we act. It's our experiences and environment that shapes us. For example, if you grow up in an extremely poor area with lots of crime, your chances of becoming a criminal go through the roof, regardless of what your race is.

The first step to a resolution or conversation is finding common ground and understanding where they come from.

They say to not judge a book by its cover. But as humans, we all think that we are great judges of character and people's intelligence. I'm guilty of it myself. Yet, I can't tell you how many times I did or said something dumb. I can only imagine if someone got a glimpse of those moments alone without context. Oh, how stupid I would look. I would be the next thing getting cancelled. No one would want to read this book. But luckily, at least with those closest to us, we get many chances at redeeming ourselves. For years, we get to build our social resume and present a better picture of our overall abilities. But with most people, we have no such rapport. We judge and we get judged on small, insignificant moments.

If you truly understand this, you will stress less and have more meaningful interactions every time. Every interaction will look like an opportunity, instead of a negative experience. You will have more friends, land more sales, and be happier. To have humility and empathy is to free yourself from the burden of negativity.

HAPPINESS LIES IN THE MIDDLE

We are constantly at odds with ourselves, pulled in opposite directions by two powerful forces. On the one hand, we are driven to strive, to achieve and to try harder. On the other, we are urged to slow down, appreciate what we have and relax. We are all too familiar with this tug-of-war.

It can be hard to stay content for too long. We often put too much pressure on ourselves, punishing ourselves for not having done enough. Have you ever asked yourself why you don't have the job of your dreams? Or why you don't have someone special in your life? Or why you haven't achieved financial success? Or why you haven't taken the steps to pursue your aspirations? Or why others don't seem to recognize your accomplishments?

THE METHOD

We are constantly bombarded by this strong force, one stemming deep from our insecurities, our need for approval, and social norms - a force which is only strengthened by social media. Our feelings of success feel like small breaths of air while otherwise drowning in our inadequacy and disappointment. We often give ourselves only moments to be proud and happy of our accomplishments, yet we allow ourselves to linger endlessly in our misery. No matter what we achieve, it's never good enough; someone has always done it better. And whatever we get, we always want something more. The present always pales in comparison to our past and the potential future.

The other force slows us down. When we push ourselves too hard, we blame ourselves for living in a state of constant stress. We may ask ourselves: why am I always angry? Why do I hate my life? Why don't I have time for the things and people I love? Why am I always tired? Why can't I enjoy all the things I have? We are blessed with opportunities, yet cursed by the ever-moving hands of time. We may listen to our body or mind, slow down, and do nothing at all. But then we once again punish ourselves for not doing anything. It's a vicious cycle and one of the hardest battles of all: a battle with ourselves.

If there is a unifying theme in The Method, it is balance - within ourselves, in our choices, in our actions, and in our perceptions. It forces us to confront difficult emotions while recognizing that sometimes we must make tough decisions, even if it means temporarily sacrificing the good for the bad. When we learn to master this balance, life can become a beautiful symphony. That is why The Method is so important; it is a simple tool that helps us to identify and address our inner needs, enabling us to take better care of our mental health and ultimately live happier lives.

Another realization that usually only comes later in life is that you can pretty much do anything in moderation. If you have the self-control and balance, you can enjoy all the forbidden delights that life has to offer. It's a liberating thought. When something is presented as purely good or bad, it rarely is. How many times has it turned out that something that was supposed to be good for you, turned out to be bad? And vice versa? Anything can have negative effects in excess, whether it be whisky, celery, or even sleep.

As the United States underwent rapid industrialization in the late 1800s, its diet underwent a dramatic transformation. Many people had relocated to cities for employment, making it necessary to deliver food from farms located outside of town. Unfortunately, due to a lack of modern refrigeration, food was spoiling quickly. Luckily, scientists had begun to develop a new field of preservatives, allowing food to stay fresh longer. Although this was very beneficial, Americans were now consuming potentially dangerous preservatives such as borax, formaldehyde and salicylic acid at an alarming rate, without having any knowledge of the effects these compounds could have on their health.

Harvey Washington Wiley, a farm boy turned chemist, questioned the effects of the newly available preservatives. He took a job with the U.S. Department of Agriculture and began the controversial Hygienic Table Trials. This grueling experiment required 12 young and healthy government employees to take capsules of preservatives such as borax and formaldehyde alongside their meals. After five years of this gruesome trial, Wiley gathered enough evidence to prove that these preservatives were dangerous. This shocking discovery led to the passing of the 1906 Pure Food and Drug Act, which later paved the way for the creation of the U.S. Food and Drug Administration (FDA). [39][40][41] It serves as a not-so-subtle reminder to always be mindful of the things we consume and put in our bodies.

A less-discussed side of this experiment is the fact that our bodies are incredible machines, with the ability to withstand unimaginable punishment and to balance themselves out. This experiment demonstrated the remarkable resilience of our bodies, as participants ingested copious amounts of poisonous substances. While they were closely monitored and the experiment was halted as soon as someone could no longer go on, it was still an incredible feat that demonstrated the power of human endurance.

Our bodies are incredibly strong and resilient. When we maintain a good balance between the good and the bad, and pay attention to our body's warning signs, we can effectively lead normal and healthy lives. Genetics, of course, also play a role in our health, and there may be exceptions to this. However, our obsession with cleanliness and diets can be unnecessary and, sometimes, even dangerous.

HOW TO GET ANYTHING YOU WANT: THE POWER OF ASKING

Some people work hard for it, some people just ask for it. You have no idea the things that you can get by simply asking for them. You also have no idea what you have missed out by not asking. I have lowered my bills; gotten free food, concert tickets, electronics, and autographs; gotten into VIP areas, received dates, free trips, hotel stays, and countless other things – simply by asking. Being personable and charming definitely will help your case. But there's a way to enhance the chances of your success even more. Studies show that simply asking for something and adding "because ______" at the end of it will improve the odds that the person will grant your request. [42]

As kids, we are always asking for things. I remember asking not only my parents but even strangers for the most ridiculous stuff. Can I sit in the one of a kind vehicle at a car show? Can I try some of that dessert that you are having? As a kid, my success rate was through the roof. While being a cute kid definitely gives you a leg up and people are more willing to give you what you want, it doesn't change too much as an adult. If you are nice enough about it, most people are willing to make exceptions and to help.

One of my first experiences in asking for something was when I thought my phone bill was too high. I called up my provider and asked them if there is anything they could do about it. After a talk with a supervisor, they lowered my bill by 15%. The entire call from beginning to end took nine minutes. I am still enjoying those discounts to this day.

I thought that this may have been a fluke. You know, a situation where they don't want to lose a "loyal" customer so they would rather offer you a discounted service. But I quickly found out that this was the rule, not the exception.

At first, I was cautious and picky about what I asked for. Then some of my requests became absurd. I've heard "no" more times than I can count, but I've also heard "yes" more than I would've ever imagined.

To ask for something, first, identify what it is that you want. Then, understand why you actually want it. Identify someone who has the power to give you what you want. Be direct and ask for what you want. That's all there is to it.

Jia Jang, the author of *Rejection Proof*, discovered the power of asking. By asking for things and being constantly rejected he learned to get over his fears. More importantly, it led to some unforgettable experiences.

On one occasion, Jang went to the University of Texas at Austin, knocked on professors' doors, and asked them if he could teach their class. The first two rightfully denied his request. But to his bewilderment, the third teacher took him up on his request and told him he'd fit him into his curriculum in a few months. After teaching it, he cried and reflected, "I used to think I had to accomplish all these things -- have to be a great entrepreneur, or get a PhD to teach -- but no, I just asked, and I could teach."

On other occasions, he was allowed to play soccer in someone's backyard, fly a stranger's aircraft, and even drive a police car.

I know, introverts are already shaking at the prospect of talking to somebody, but it's possible. I was much braver when I was young. As I got into my teenage years and even well into my 20s, I had significant trouble in interacting with people. I avoided phone calls with strangers at all costs (and to be honest, sometimes I still do). I was too afraid to ask even for the most basic things, like directions to the bathroom. I would've rather had my bladder explode while I tried to find the toilet on my own than talk to someone. But over the past few years, I've learned to use digital communication. Chat and e-mail communication became my go-to methods for dealing with the outside world. But I knew in order to grow and experience new things, I needed to learn to communicate with people and overcome this anxiety. Social anxiety is a serious issue that deserves more than a paragraph to be addressed. But from personal experience, slowly putting myself in situations where I am uncomfortable helped me to get over it.

LOCATION, LOCATION, LOCATION

To be productive and to succeed, you need to be not only in the right mind state but also in the right environment. I found that after years of working from home, my house wasn't the best location for optimal productivity. It is too easy to get distracted and since I happen to be at home, everyone assumes I am free all the time. I am also only steps away from the kitchen, the telephone, and any visitors.

So if you work remotely, going to a cafe, or even out to nature may boost your productivity tenfold. I found myself completing a day's worth of work in a few hours in the right environment. Now, how about if you are stuck in your office cubicle? Or perhaps you don't have the choice of a location in your job? In that case, you have two choices. To make the best out of your location and to optimize it, or to change your location altogether. I am not talking about hopping from one job to another, but to physically move. To relocate to a different city, state, or even country. As ridiculous as it sounds, this is something everyone should consider.

Typically, our location is chosen by our parents. We are born where we are born, and we tend to remain in the same area. We may move to a bigger city nearby, but usually, our environment, where we spend all our lives, is chosen by someone else. Yet the people in the area may not be the most open-minded. Or maybe it's always cloudy. There could be a lack of nature. There may be various other reasons why the environment is not suitable for you. How can you thrive in this kind of environment and be content?

The more we wait, the more intertwined and invested we get in our environment and the harder it becomes to change it. People say dismissively that the grass is always greener on the other side. However, sometimes it is. Moving is actually one of the top fears for most people. More accurately it is metathesiophobia, or a fear of change. But it isn't something that we should fear. The only constant in life is change. We are constantly changing and so is our environment.

THE METHOD

If you stay in the same spot long enough, you'll see how life doesn't stop for you and everything around you changes. Why shouldn't you change too? But you'll also notice that you could spend the next 20 years of your life doing exactly what you've been doing in the last 20. You'll be with the same friends, have the same job, take the same routes, with very minor changes. If you are happy where you are, that's great news. If not, well, you understand. Also, realize that moving doesn't have to be permanent. You can change your home and location more than once; and most likely, you will. But you don't have to wait to have a family to do that. In fact, your significant other might be waiting for you in another city—or even on the other side of the world.

Although a lot is involved in moving, it allows us to start fresh and activates our brain. It's a chance to reassess aspects of your life and routine you may not have considered in a long while. It makes us figure things out in a way that's best for us, not everyone else. You can finally organize the life the way you wanted, not what someone else chose for you. Another reason to consider moving is that some places are simply better environments.

According to the world happiness report, which surveys people about their life satisfaction, there are some countries that consistently rank at the top for overall happiness. Economic, government and social factors all play roles in determining the score. If you have the opportunity to try living in any one of those countries and fit in, why wouldn't you try? Of course, don't forget to consider your family and friends - your social cup should never be empty!

FIND YOUR REASON FOR BEING

From a young age, we're often asked what we want to be in life. While the answer may come easy when we're young (astronaut, anyone?), the question can become increasingly daunting as we enter high school, college, and even our 40s. Our childhood aspirations often dwindle as life goes on, leaving us feeling a disconnect between our abilities, desires, and what the world actually needs. Wouldn't it be great if there was a course in school that could help us figure out the answer to that question and give us some direction in life? Since there isn't, The Method can help us balance our lives and get us where we want to go. But first, it's important to have a general sense of what you want and where you're heading.

There's a Japanese concept called Ikigai. It means "a reason for being." We all need to find this within our lives. There's a powerful exercise that helps you find your Ikigai. It's not an end goal, but rather a general path. Ikigai helps balance your needs with the needs of the world. Just like The Method, it's not as philosophical and complex as it sounds. It's four easy steps, and it's worth giving it a shot in any stage of life.

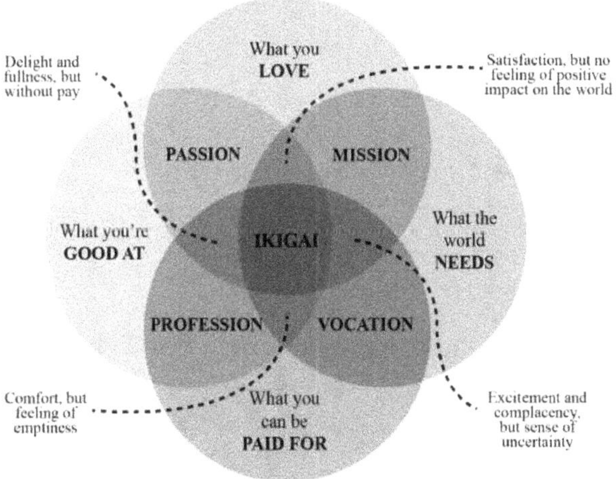

As pictured above, it is usually done by drawing four overlapping circles, but I find it easier to use squares. You simply divide a sheet of paper into four even sections. Starting from the top left section, write down the following headers going counterclockwise. The first section is "What do you love?" The second is "What are you good at?" The third is "What can you get paid for"? The final section is "What does the world need?" Next, you will fill out those sections and answer the questions. The goal is to write whatever comes to mind without overthinking.[43] Each section should take only about 3-5 minutes. To help you get started here are some questions to think about for each of the sections.

What do you love?

-What do you never get bored of?

-What is something that you're always drawn back to?

-What gets you into a zone, to the point where you forget to drink and eat?

It really can be anything, it doesn't have to be realistic. Perhaps you love to doodle or enjoy deep conversations. Write this down!

What are you good at?

-What do people ask for your help with?

-What do others tell you that you are good at?

-What skills have you been practicing?

-Is there something that you want to be good at?

What can you get paid for?

-What would you do if you weren't in your current job?

-What have you been paid for before?

-What do you want to get paid for?

What does the world need?

-How are the people like and what do they need?

-What could you contribute to affect those around you in a positive way?

-What would be useful to people right now? Is there something you can improve?

Usually this is the part that people find the hardest. So instead of thinking about the planet as a whole, maybe you can think about your own world instead. Your immediate community and society. Maybe it's broad, like having less stress, or specific, like reducing the workload of doctors and nurses so they make fewer mistakes.

Once you have filled out all the sections, see if there is anything you want to add. Then, you can move on to the most fun part: finding your Ikigai or purpose. Circle and find something common from all four sections. If you cannot find something common in all four sections, think if there is a job you can create that combines things from each of the sections. For example, let's suppose you love muffins, are good at making videos, have gotten paid for babysitting, and your world could use more teachers. In that case, maybe you could teach children the fundamentals of cooking and making desserts.

Albert Einstein was a major proponent of combinatory play as a means of discovering innovative ideas. By blending seemingly unrelated things such as music, art, and ideas, he was able to come up with the famous equation E=MC2. As he said, "Combinatory play seems to be the essential feature in productive thought".[46] When we limit ourselves with guidelines, rules, and achievements of others, our vision is narrowed and we are unable to explore the unexpected, which can lead to interesting ideas. When considering your own Ikigai, it is important to think outside of the box and be spontaneous. You never know what you might discover when you do!

But for some of you, it may not be that easy. It may take days or even months. And that's okay. Finding your Ikigai is an ongoing process. The important thing is to enjoy the process as much as the goal. As I mentioned before, we all have a finite amount of effort and time. Whether you spend it in tasks you dislike, or in a balanced and fulfilling lifestyle, is up to you.

Just like The Method, your answers may also change as you and your life evolve. Your reason for being may also change over time. But it will help you find a general path that will lead to new experiences. It will allow you to follow something with more passion, instead of working towards a dead-end goal or fulfilling someone else's dreams.

Finding ways to spend your time more enjoyably can actually give you more of it. To find the answer on how to live longer, researchers pinpointed five zones where people live the longest, called the "Blue Zones." These rare spots are where people seem to thrive into their hundreds. One of these Blue Zones is Okinawa, Japan. During his TED Talk "How to Live to Be 100+," National Geographic reporter Dan Buettner suggested Ikigai as one of the potential explanations for longevity.[44] Many have tried to study and understand what makes regions like these so special, and what they constantly come back to is a sense of purpose and community.[45] It is not the only reason, but it is a common factor, and another reason for you to find your purpose and move toward it.

THE ART OF SELLING: CRAFTING A POSITIVE PERCEPTION

No matter the occasion, appearance is everything. Whether you are attending a job interview, going on a date, or attempting to sneak into somewhere, the way you look matters. Professionalism and neatness can open many doors, but appearance extends beyond just how you dress. Presentation is equally as important when presenting a school project, a new product for work, or giving a gift. Sometimes, the presentation of something matters more than the actual item itself. For example, imagine giving someone a movie ticket as their birthday present. By itself, this may be an ordinary and uninteresting gift. However, if you present it in an eye-catching way, such as in a beautiful envelope with a personalized note, it can then become something worth talking about.

Perception can be more influential than reality; this is exemplified by the initial flop of cake mixes. Housewives felt that using a cake mix would be cheating on cooking, so they refused to purchase them. However, a genius idea changed the perception of cake mixes: adding an egg. This small change was enough to convince customers to buy them, making them wildly successful. Similarly, car doors are designed to close with a loud thud to make you feel more secure. User interface designers often add loading animations to websites and apps to give the impression that the product is more sophisticated. Ultimately, it's all about providing the expected experience.

People often feel like a product isn't really doing anything unless they can see some kind of process in action. This is why manufacturers add foaming agents to modern cleaning products – the bubbles give us the impression that something is happening. Apple Music had to make their random music function less random, as users felt that having the same artist come up several times in a row wasn't random enough. To address this, they adjusted the algorithm so that it wouldn't pick songs by the same artist consecutively. Vacuum cleaners and microwaves often make loud and exaggerated noises to make them seem more powerful – all this is just a ploy to get us to buy more and feel more comfortable. It turns out that simply changing the perception of a product is often enough to convince people to do what you want.

Appearance can be a powerful tool. It can make or break the impressions we give people, and it can be used to manipulate our perception of a product. In the end, it is important to remember that it's not always about how something actually is but rather how it is presented.

THE STRENGTH OF ASKING FOR HELP

Don't be afraid to reach out for help – it can be a life-altering decision. I used to think that I could handle everything on my own, never asking for support, guidance, or even a different point of view. I'm not sure if I was too proud to be vulnerable, or if I thought I knew everything, or if I didn't want to put my problems on other people; but, I now know that asking for help can be incredibly rewarding. My friends and family were more than happy to lend a hand, and even my social media followers provided some valuable insights. Not only did people jump at the chance to lend a hand, but it also made them feel good knowing they were able to help. Just be cautious when it comes to asking for money - that's a whole different ballgame.

Arnold Schwarzenegger came to America with only $20 to his name. However, when he tells his story of success, he does not consider himself self-made. He states, "It is not true that I am self-made. Like everyone, to get to where I am, I stood on the shoulders of giants. My life was built on a foundation of parents, coaches, and teachers; of kind souls who lent couches or gym back rooms where I could sleep; of mentors who shared wisdom and advice; of idols who motivated me from the pages of magazines (and, as my life grew, from personal interaction). I had a big vision, and I had a fire in my belly. But I would never have gotten anywhere without my mother helping me with my homework (and smacking me when I wasn't ready to study), without my father telling me to 'be useful,' without teachers who explained how to sell, or without coaches who taught me the fundamentals of weight lifting."[47]

Schwarzenegger is being remarkably candid about his past; most autobiographies and self-help books by people touting their success as models for others will not mention the shoulders of giants on which they too stood. Instead, they usually credit their success to themselves. It is important to not forget to ask for help and to never forget those who have helped you along the way.

> *"If you want to go fast, go alone, if you want to go far, go together"*
>
> – UNKNOWN

JUST DO IT: TAKE A NAP

If you watch any movie, read any motivational book, they all tell you to go get it. Go into gear and never stop! Wake up at 6am, or better yet, never sleep! In real life, that's unsustainable in the long run. And in most cases, impossible. Life has setbacks;

we have to deal with all kinds of distractions, including our own lazy personalities. Not to mention the fact that our brains and bodies need rest to function at their highest levels. Humans are amazing machines, but we just aren't built to run at top efficiency all the time.

For centuries, companies have worked their workers until exhaustion. It took many years for them to humanize working conditions and accept the 40-hour week. It's taken them another 100 years to realize that even that is too much. Smart companies today are once again reducing work weeks and increasing breaks. This has been shown to increase the productivity[48][49], longevity[50], and happiness of its employees. Go figure – allow people to work less and they'll accomplish more.

But we don't all control our work hours. So I'd like to address something you can control: **taking breaks, naps**, and **meditating**. Allowing yourself to take a 10-minute break in each hour worked will allow you to be more productive and focused. It's true that you may not be able to do this in a job where continuous physical labor is involved. But it is certainly doable in an office job where you can seem like you are working on something, when in fact, you are enjoying the bliss of nothingness.

Not many of us are allowed actual napping on the job, although it's getting more prevalent around the world. Especially Japan. For years, the grueling work culture has taken a toll on its workers. But recently, some companies in Japan started incorporating midday naps in order to increase productivity. In fact, sleep cafes have sprung up all over Japan in order to help groggy workers enjoy a better quality of life. [51]

For 750-yen ($6.90), workers can get a coffee and 30 minutes of shuteye. Naps can enhance performance, increase alertness, and reduce mistakes. And it's not just the overworked countries that can benefit from naps. You can too. In the '80s and '90s NASA and FAA were trying to find out whether in-cockpit naps could improve the safety for pilots flying long-haul routes. They found a 40-minute nap improved the performance of their pilots by 34% and physiological alertness by 100% compared to their non-napping counterparts.[52] The sweet spot for a nap appears to be around 20 minutes with an ideal time to nap between 1:00 p.m. - 4:00 p.m. [53][54]

TURN A DAILY CHORE INTO A POWERFUL TOOL FOR SELF-IMPROVEMENT

Although every one of us enters this planet breathing – it's pretty much the first thing every one of us does when we're born – this subconscious process is largely ignored. We give breathing very little thought and we continue to breathe when we are asleep or even unconscious. It would seem counterproductive to disrupt this natural and automatic process. But that's exactly what every one of us needs to do.

If I told you someone scaled Mount Kilimanjaro in nothing but shorts and ran a full marathon in the Namib desert without drinking anything, you'd probably think I was talking about someone superhuman. The man behind those achievements is Wim Hof. For many years, people have tried to figure out what makes his body so special. Perhaps it was his genetics, the fact he was Dutch, or something unique in his body. However, for just as many years, Wim Hof has spent trying to tell people that he was the same as all of us. What does he credit his incredible abilities to? Breathing. Well, not just breathing. Wim Hof has a method of his own that combines breathing, cold exposure, and meditation.

THE METHOD

But how is Wim Hof different from other gurus, businessmen, and inspirational figures? Those who achieve something great, then profit from products that supposedly give us a path to do the same. After all, as I pointed out above, the reason why most of your diets and plans to get rich will fail is that each person's case is unique. Wim Hof is different because his method is science-based and replicable by anyone. Since 2007, Wim Hof has taken part in various studies that have proven the effectiveness of his methods and that others can follow them to obtain similar results. Who wouldn't want to be able to withstand extreme temperatures, control their body's immune response, or improve their overall happiness? According to those who studied Wim Hof, you can. Through breathing, cold exposure, and meditation.

Researchers were initially skeptical of Hof and considered his methods to be pseudoscience. However, Hof voluntarily sought out researchers who would be willing to test him. After taking part in several studies, he shocked the researchers by proving that he was able to voluntarily influence his autonomic nervous system. Until that point, this was thought to be impossible. What's more, is that he was able to take 12 practitioners of his method and have them replicate his success in influencing the nervous system and immune system response. Since then, he has taken part in eight other studies that confirmed the effectiveness of his method. [55][56]

I struggled with my immune system for years. When I was younger, I was sick all the time. I would miss many fun summers, looking out the window and watching my friends playing outside while I laid in bed with a fever. At one point, my parents were so desperate they sent me to a health clinic for a week. However, this did little to improve my health. In fact, the drugs I was prescribed made it even worse. It was then that my parents started learning about natural methods for healing and improving the immune system.

When I got sick, they would make herbal teas, soups, and even pour buckets of cold water over me to reduce my fever. At one point, I remember they took me to a polar bear plunge. This is where people voluntarily go into freezing water in their underwear. It took the 8-year-old me all of five seconds in that water to decide I never wanted to do that again. But somehow, the various methods seemed to be helping. I was still getting sick, but not as often. Over time, I became a normal human being. I was getting sick no more often than anyone else.

Looking back on it now, my parents had the right idea. Cold exposure, a good diet, and exercise are all things that still keep me healthy today. Albeit, dumping buckets of freezing water while I am sick wasn't good timing and probably made things worse. But turns out, that cold exposure at the right time helps to train our bodies, and it's something I utilize now. But I want to give you the absolute simplest ways with the biggest effects.

This is why I always recommend the Wim Hof Method to all my friends. For the last year, I have been doing breathing and cold exposure techniques. Although I had some sniffles or a cough here and there, I haven't had any real downtime being sick while using his method. I feel like I can tolerate heat and cold much better. I feel a lot happier and less stressed. In fact, I have replaced my daily meditation with breathing techniques from WHM. I incorporate WHM in The Method in my self-improvement section every day. It takes 15 minutes each day. 5 of those minutes I spend taking a cold shower. I started with warm water, and then gradually moved to the coldest setting in your shower. I worked my way up from 30 seconds to 5 minutes until I no longer use any warm water whatsoever. I do this every morning to energize myself. Then, I use another ten minutes to do breathing techniques. I lay down comfortably. I inhale deeply through the nose (you can do it through the mouth as well) and exhale unforced through the mouth. I fully inhale through the belly, then chest and then let go unforced. I repeat this 30 to 40 times. Then, on the final breath, after exhaling, I hold my breath for two minutes or until I feel I need to breathe. Then, I take a deep breath and hold it for 15 seconds. I repeat this cycle three times. Instantly, I feel all my anxiety is gone and I feel completely relaxed. It is an incredibly small investment and requires just 15 minutes a day, but the payoff is astronomical.

There are getaways, drugs, and courses that cost tens of thousands of dollars that seek to accomplish what these few things do for free. Wim Hof has social media accounts where you can follow along for free. These are the types of things I could leave out of this book and credit all of my successes to The Method. However, my goal is to give you all the necessary ingredients to make you flourish. Nothing is left out, even if that means promoting a method within The Method.

Even if you don't plan to climb Everest in your shorts and the Wim Hof method seems like more than you want to try, focused breathing for ten minutes a day is a scientifically proven and simple way to improve your quality of life. I can't think of many things that offer more value without cost or side effects. Breathing, meditation, and cold exposure should be in everyone's daily habit arsenal.

THE HIGH COST OF BEING TOO HUMBLE

The terms "con-artist" and "con-man" have a long and storied history, beginning with Samuel Thompson, the original "confidence man" of the early 1800s. Thompson was a crook who asked his victims to give him money or their watches, instead of gaining their confidence first. Despite being unsuccessful, Thompson was viewed as a genius due to a misunderstanding of a satirical article about his arrest by the New York Herald. [57] This misunderstanding led the term "confidence man" to stick and be used to describe anyone who gains someone's trust and then persuades them to do or believe something false.

Frank Abagnale was an impressive con-man, and his schemes were truly remarkable. He began his criminal career with a series of bank frauds, including forging checks and depositing personal checks on his own overdrawn account. But perhaps his most daring feat was the simplest: he magnetically printed his own account number on blank deposit slips, and mixed them in with the real ones at the bank. Anyone depositing money at the bank would be in for a surprise when their money ended up in Abagnale's account. [58]

Abagnale also devised a clever plan to get his hands on money from airline and car rental companies. He purchased a security guard uniform from a costume shop, put up a sign outside the drop box that said "Out of Service - Place Deposits with the Security Guard on Duty," and collected the money himself. To his astonishment, he was successful. He was later quoted saying: "How can a dropbox be out of service?" [59]

Throughout his career, Abagnale assumed no less than 8 identities, including an airline pilot, a lawyer, a physician, and a U.S. Bureau of Prisons agent. His story was made into a movie in 2002, titled "Catch Me if You Can." [60][61][62]

It's not just random folks who fall victim to these con artists. In 2008, a scheme unraveled that was so big, that it is unlikely ever to be repeated. Thousands of sophisticated hedge funds, charities, and Hollywood stars lost billions of dollars in a decades-long scheme. He lured them in with consistently high profits, using profits from new investors to pay off old ones. While Madoff seemed to be unimpeachable, things started to unravel when investors requested to withdraw their money due to growing suspicions and the financial crisis. Madoff was eventually caught and sentenced to 150 years in prison.

At the time of his arrest, he was astonished that the SEC failed to expose his fraud. He said there had been two occasions when they were a step away from catching him red-handed. However, due to negligence, reputation, and various other factors, the scheme was able to stay afloat. [63] Madoff's calm demeanor and confidence were a crucial factor in his ability to keep the fraud going. In the end, $65 billion vanished into thin air.

Rather than glorifying criminal behavior, the stories of these con-artists should serve to illustrate the power of self-confidence. We are often too humble or shy to ask for what we deserve, so we settle for less than our worth. But it is important to remember that society is hard-wired to accept brash confidence as a sign of competence. Therefore, sometimes it pays to "fake it 'til you make it".

There are many people out there whose success is largely attributed to their self-confidence and boldness in asking for what they want. On the other hand, you may feel apprehensive about asking for a raise or speaking up in order to avoid potential conflict. When you do accomplish something, you may not take the time to be proud of yourself because you think it's not as impressive as someone else's successes. You may even let yourself get taken advantage of in relationships because you're scared to stand up for yourself. Being humble is commendable, but there are moments when it's important to recognize and appreciate your own accomplishments. Don't make yourself out to be less than you are - instead, present yourself as a beautiful gift to the world that you are. Present yourself as more, not less.

CONCLUSION:

Implement these into your life to achieve what you want faster and easier.

CHAPTER NINE

CHANGE YOUR DEFINITION OF SUCCESS

The Method works because you're focusing on smaller, achievable tasks in areas of your life that are important. In other words, you're redefining what it means to finish your to-do list in order to succeed. This principle can be extended to the rest of your life as well. Something that gets lost while in pursuit of something better is appreciating what you already have. Frequently we compare ourselves to others and the glamour around us. The love stories, the material possessions, and other things we call "success." Thanks to social media, we have access to millions of people's lives at our fingertips. Bombarded by carefully curated stimuli designed to convince you to envy people and want things, it's becoming incredibly difficult just to appreciate what you have. People always present the best versions of themselves and their lives online.

It's easy to get caught up in comparing ourselves to others. There's always someone more successful than us, doing something more interesting. We often find ourselves looking at everyone else's plate, wondering if their portion is bigger than ours. But instead of focusing on what others have, let's take some time to appreciate the abundance we have in front of us. Instead of worrying about what we don't have, let's focus on becoming the best versions of ourselves, and celebrating our successes along the way. Remember, the only reason we should be looking at someone else's plate is to make sure they have enough. If we focus on what truly matters to us, financial success will come.

Fill a room with a thousand people and ask how many consider themselves lucky. Likely, only a few will raise their hands. Perhaps they just got a promotion or had a baby. But, for the most part, many people do not consider themselves lucky. They reflect upon the flat tire they got, the time their boss yelled at them, or the fact that they are generally unhappy.

However, these same people hope to turn it around for themselves, and to do so quickly and without effort. How do we know this? Let's take the most obvious example: the lottery. Being killed by a vending machine, struck by lightning, or becoming the President of the United States - what do these things have in common? The chances of having these things happen in one's lifetime are much higher than those of winning a major lottery. For instance, the odds of winning the second-largest Mega Millions jackpot were 1 in 259,000,000. Despite this, many people will quickly give up the hope of achieving their dreams or becoming the President, yet they will gladly take these odds in the hopes of becoming rich overnight. In fact, those earning less than $13,000 per year spend approximately 9% of their income on lottery tickets.

So here's my point: imagine you won the lottery, and you were once again in the same room. You are asked the same question. You would raise your hand now, right? What if I told you, *you've already won the lottery*? Again, again and again. Not a lottery with prize money, but an incredible lottery nonetheless. The simple fact that you are here reading this very book and breathing means you are already the product of trillions of "coincidences" that combined at the exact right time to produce you. The odds that your parents met, found each other attractive, continued to stay together, and decided to have you is 1 in 40,000,000. Not too bad. Now, the odds of being exactly who you are (a particular egg, meeting a specific sperm) is 1 in 400 *quadrillion*. Try typing that number out. This also means that every single one of your ancestors had also had to beat similar odds, making your odds of existence even worse.

So considering all these factors, take a guess what your chances are of even existing? **Zero**. (Or as close to zero as it's possible to get.)[75] The mathematical odds tell us that you should not exist in this little universe of ours. Yet there you are, sitting and breathing. You've hit the lottery. You've hit it many times.

But maybe you don't feel lucky. After all, you don't have possessions that many other people have. Maybe so, but if you have food in your fridge, clothes on your back, a roof over your head, and a place to sleep, you have more than 75% of the world. According to The World Bank, nearly half the world lives on less than $5.50 a day.[64] But money isn't the same thing as happiness. I have personally seen some of the happiest people in third-world countries. I have seen children whose parents couldn't afford to buy them shoes who were as happy as any child I've seen. Conversely, I have met some of the most miserable people with watches on their wrist that could pay someone's annual salary. It's all about perspective.

If you're hungry and you find yourself with a plate of food, you're likely to feel joyful - until you see someone with two plates. Even though you likely have enough food to feed two, you become so focused on the fact that someone else has more that you forget to enjoy what's on your plate. Instead of feeling content, you may experience greed, anger, and even disappointment. This simple example serves as a reminder of how our world turns.

Parents work tirelessly to ensure their children won't have to experience the same hardships they did. They take on two jobs, hire a babysitter and live a high-stress lifestyle - all in the name of providing for their kids. But is it really worth it?

What is most important for a child? Their parents. And what's missing? Parents spending quality time with their kids.

We all want to provide our children with the best. We want to get a better job to pay for a better car or a better home. But it will never be enough. It's time to recognize that the most precious commodity in the world - our time - is being spent on things that don't really matter.

Yes, we need food and shelter, and we need to work to get them. However, let's remember Maslov's pyramid - success is not what the media tells us it is. Investing time and energy into our relationships with our children is the key to true happiness.

No matter how much or how little money you have, becoming rich starts with defining what success means to you. The media may portray success as having a large house, throwing opulent parties, driving a luxury car, and being in the spotlight. But to me, these are just compensations for not being truly happy. Many of those who have achieved this level of wealth have done so by investing their most valuable and scarce commodity – time – into accumulating a large amount of money. In their pursuit of riches, they have often had to sacrifice their childhoods, trample on their friends and colleagues, and miss out on opportunities to grow as individuals and become more compassionate. They may know how to work hard, but their efforts are not necessarily focused on making the world a better place.

True success is simpler than we think: **it's about being happy and making others happy**. I don't think anyone needs a yacht or a $2000 purse to be happy. The whole "I'd rather sleep in a Ferrari than on the street" concept is nonsense. No one wants to live on the street, but no one would have to if we placed the same importance on everyone's needs. What if you gave a portion of your plate to feed another, instead of looking at someone else's plate? What if we defined success as being happy and making others happy? If you spend your whole life trying to achieve someone else's definition of success, you will never achieve your own. That is why only you can decide which categories are important to include on your Method Day planner. Only you can define what success looks like for you.

What does it mean to be rich? It's the feeling of being in the here and now, of making a difference in the world and of being healthy. It's spending your days on activities that are meaningful and having a support system when you stumble. It's being generous and giving more than you take. But wealth doesn't always equate to a monetary figure. If Forbes truly assessed wealth in this way, how many people would be on the world's richest list? Could you be one of them?

CONCLUSION:

Understand that money is a tool. It's not a measurement for success or happiness. Change the way you think of success and pursue things that matter to you. Monetary success will follow.

CHAPTER TEN

THREE TRAITS SHARED BY SUCCESSFUL PEOPLE

Once you understand what it means to be truly rich, your perspective will shift and you'll see people differently. You'll be able to look past the media and see that there are rich people all around you. You will notice they tend to share three traits that draw people in and make them successful in their ventures. Just by noticing these traits, you can learn from others and become more successful yourself. If you learn these three valuable traits, you'll not only elevate yourself but those around you as well. They will pay dividends in business and beyond.

I. POSITIVITY & KINDNESS

Some people apply the airplane rule (put on your own oxygen mask before assisting others) when it comes to their life. The truth is, you don't have to have much or even feel good to be kind to others. We often use our mood, our circumstances, and our economic position as an excuse as to why we are rude to others. It's an easy out. But we must understand that kind words, hugs, listening, love, or a smile don't cost anything. You don't need to pretend that everything is okay in your life to be kind. You can summon the strength to be kind in whatever position you may be.

It's often the people that are in the worst situations who are the kindest. Why? Because they have compassion and understand what effect the smallest gestures can have. But what's in it for you? We've already talked about how giving pays. Well, when you are kind and positive, it's been proven to transform your brain physically. It also attracts positivity from others. What you give in kindness, you usually get back tenfold. Forcing your mind to be positive and faking a smile may seem silly, but it has been proven to improve your mood and boost your immune system.[65][66] It's also a way to break out of the cycle of misery. Have you ever complimented someone, and watched them explode with joy? That energy is contagious, and it will change both of your days. It will impact the rest of the people they interact with that day and from then on. Positivity and kindness are somethings that successful people share.

2. PERSISTENCE

Most "success" books will tell you to never give up. That hard work and never giving up are the keys to success. For the record, I don't agree. While it's important to have a strong work ethic, you should always choose to work smart over hard (remember?). 20% of your effort yields 80% of your results, right? Why not focus on that 20%? And as for never giving up, there are plenty of times you should give up. That's why you start your daily planner fresh every day: you need to decide, based on your own categories and your own priorities, what you need to carry over from day to day.

Oftentimes, people fall into the "sunk cost fallacy." We'd like to think we make rational decisions based on the future value of objects, investments, and experiences. But the truth is that our choices are usually tainted by our emotional investment. The more emotional investment we have in something, the harder it becomes to abandon it. Think of your past relationship. The more time you spent with someone, the more emotional investment you had, the harder it became to end the relationship, even if all the red flags were there. But this is not limited to relationships. If you worked for ten years in setting up a business, regardless of its success or failure, you will be unlikely to abandon it no matter what happens. You've worked too hard for it. The truth is, there are many cases in which we need to either reevaluate our strategies and redistribute our efforts, or give up on something altogether.

While knowing when to call it quits matters, that doesn't mean that persistence isn't important. Can you recall asking for a gift from your parents for your birthday or Christmas? They may have said no at first. But being a kid, you asked 20 more times until you got what you wanted. While it's a childish example, that's the kind of persistence we lack as adults. We accept rejections and give up on things that matter to us too quickly. We give up on potential relationships, jobs, deals, and making our dreams come true because we are not persistent enough. Yet, being persistent is not just asking something multiple times or attempting something more than once. It's continuously showing up, improving, adjusting, and trying again.

Why does it work? People's circumstances and emotions change. When you inquired about something the first time, they may have been experiencing a terrible day. If you ask at a different time, they might be in an exceptionally good mood instead. Circumstances are always fluctuating. This is true not only for people, but for venues, corporations, governments, and so on.

And we usually find it admirable when people go after what they want. Imagine being a business owner. Someone you turned down for a job shows up week after week to inquire if there is a position for him. At first, you may find it funny or even annoying. But how many weeks will it take until you realize that this person has more will and perseverance than any of your employees? Even if you don't have any spots available in your company, you may want to help them out. You may point them in the right direction, refer them to your friends, or hire them in the future. Persistent people have a contagious passion. We want to be around and help people who desperately want to achieve something. Be persistent in the pursuit of your happiness.

In short, you need to be persistent when it counts, and know when to cut your losses and move on. It's something that takes practice, but when you're filling out your daily planner with The Method every day, consciously assessing what you want and need to do on levels big and small, you'll find it easier over time.

3. ADAPTABILITY

Last but not least, the most important trait of all – **adaptability**. Life will always be an unpredictable roller coaster. We can do our best to set ourselves up for success, but we will never have control over most outcomes. Unavoidably, we will find ourselves in uncomfortable situations, harmful environments, and less-than-ideal conditions. The people that get out of these situations, embrace, and even thrive in them are the ones who can adapt to their circumstances. They can adjust to and improve their environment. They figure out how to thrive in their job.

How do they do it? The right mindset. Our instinct is to complain and to indulge in self-pity in bad situations. Adaptable people, in contrast, seldom complain and understand that life circumstances are always changing. Instead, they formulate a plan to change the circumstances or find ways to make the best out of the situation. Those people won't fail in life. That might mean, as we said earlier, modifying their definition of success. Whatever life throws at them, they can adapt to it.

If you want to be successful and happy, you will have to roll with the punches. If you lose a portion of your income, adjust your lifestyle. If you are in bad company, try to bring out the best in people and be your own entertainment. If you are stuck somewhere you don't want to be, analyze your situation and make a plan to get out. If there's anything you can do about something you don't like, even if it's something small, do it. If you can't change anything, learn to live with it. It seems like common sense, but most people seem to stress over things they can't change and refuse to do anything about the things they can.

It's not just our personal lives where it's important to adapt. Business have to do the same. For example, a common household brand, Febreze, almost failed as a product. In the early 1990s, Procter & Gamble hit the jackpot. A P&G scientist was working with a substance called hydroxypropyl beta cyclodextrin (HPBCD). After he came home, his wife asked him if he had quit smoking. He hadn't. But he didn't smell like cigarettes either. Somehow this substance had made the cigarette smell disappear. He sprayed the chemical over smelly fabrics, socks, carpets, and the scent magically vanished after the mist had dried. P&G had accidentally discovered something big. They knew they had a winner.

So they spent millions in perfecting the formula and creating an odorless and colorless spray that could make a stinky jacket or couch smell like new. During the research, they came across a park ranger who was responsible for trapping skunks. Everything from her clothes to her curtains smelled of skunk. Because of this, she had no social life. She tried specialty soaps, shampoos, and everything in between. Nothing worked. But after using Febreze, the smells were gone. Almost in tears, she thanked the team for saving her love life. The story was so inspiring that company felt this product couldn't possibly fail.

They launched campaign after campaign promoting the product as an embarrassing odor eliminator…and it was a big flop.

P&G couldn't understand why its miracle product wasn't selling. They hired behavior consultants to investigate, who met with hundreds of consumers to understand how they could weave the product into everyday lives. They met one woman that used Febreze as the final touch to cleaning her rooms. She would vacuum, fluff pillows, tighten bed sheets, smile with accomplishment, and spray Febreze as the last touch. They saw the same pattern in hundreds of videotapes. So they decided to remarket Febreze as the last part of a cleaning routine. In addition, they added a distinct smell to Febreze, so consumers would be more aware of the product when they used it. Within two months, sales doubled. Now, Febreze products are responsible for 1 billion dollars in sales yearly.[67][68] Their willingness to understand their consumers and adapt was the ingredient to success.

In business terms, this is called *pivoting*. It's a sound business strategy, but it's also something that we need to utilize in our everyday lives. Just like the scent in Febreze, perhaps there's a small detail within your life that's missing, keeping you from success. Every now and then, we need to be critical of ourselves and be able to listen to feedback. This is true whether it's positive or negative. If we always insist that we are right and everyone else is wrong, we may never reach our potential.

In my own life, I had many instances where I failed to be adaptable and take advice from others. One area where asking for advice paid off for me was style. For the longest time, I wore clothes that didn't fit me well. It took me many years to realize that I wanted to look good for the opposite sex, yet the only person I'd consult on style was a male: me. The truth clicked for me when I found myself stuck between two distinctively different dress shirts. They were so different, yet in my mind, they were both equally stylish.

After 30 minutes of trying them on and failing to decide, I asked the saleswoman which one looked better. She looked at me with confusion and without hesitation, picked the smaller shirt with minimal design as if it was obvious. Then I asked another girl. And another. To them, the answer was easy. But in my mind, this was far from an easy decision. Clearly, I was missing something. After I bought the shirt, I received many compliments on it from both sexes. As a result, I became more comfortable asking for advice. Not only with clothes – with cologne, haircuts, and more. Later, this extended far beyond style.

I am now quite comfortable asking people's opinions and considering it when doing almost anything. Formerly, I was missing that outside perspective. Oftentimes, I'll pick up valuable lessons from their feedback. Perhaps there is a reason why people like one thing over another. It's a small way to be adaptable, but it made my life a whole lot easier and pleasant. It doesn't mean that you are giving up your personality or creativity, either. You can improve what you already created, or make your decision easier between things you already like. It's adapting to your circumstances, being flexible when things aren't working out, and being willing to listen.

CONCLUSION:

Be kind and surround yourself with kindness. If something matters to you, give it another shot. If you can change a situation or outcome, be methodical, and change it. If you can't, learn how to adapt.

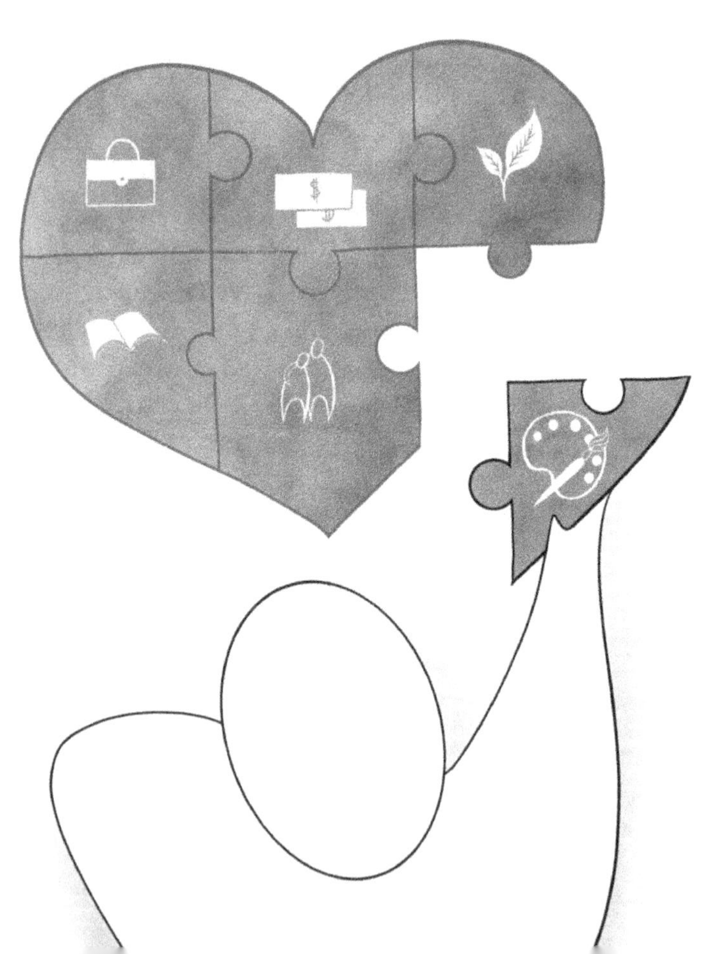

FINAL THOUGHTS

As you can see, many ingredients go into making someone successful, and there are a lot of strategies that can dramatically improve your life. You may feel overwhelmed by reading and trying to execute everything here at once. I've given you a lot to consider, but remember that this is just background and context. ***What's most important is to keep moving forward using The Method.*** The Method is about:

- Learning what your true priorities in life are

- Building your daily planner around *your* priorities and needs

- Focusing on manageable goals, one step at a time

- Refreshing and reassessing your list daily

- Taking risks

- Being adaptable

When climbers attempt to climb Mount Everest, there is no way to run up the mountain. The only way to get to the peak (and back alive) is one small step at a time. You will do the same. Rather than focusing on changing your whole life at once, focus on adding good things, one at a time, making sustainable changes and leveraging an understanding of how your mind works to steer away from harmful habits and build good ones. Before you know it, your effort will start paying dividends. You will start feeling more complete and your life trajectory will shift. As I am typing the final words to this book to help you and others, I realize how powerful this simple Method has been in transforming my own life. I hope it does the same for you.

Your accomplishments, or lack of them, don't define you. We don't share a single timeline or specific dates for each of life's events. You are not early; you are not late. **You are exactly on time.** The best time to start something was yesterday; the next best time is right now. Sure, if you're 70, you may be a bit late to begin your college basketball career…just don't tell that to Ken Mink, who sank his first points for Roane State Community College at age 73. [70]

When used daily, The Method can help improve your life. The most important thing to remember is to *keep moving forward*, no matter how small the steps. We tend to mask our self-doubt and anxiety by striving for perfection. Ironically, that's the very thing that keeps us from moving forward. As I scramble to find the perfect words to end this book, I remember that sometimes perfection lies in "good enough." Just start – a better life awaits you.

REFERENCES

[1] Susan Weinschenk Ph.D. (2019, April 19) The Science of Habits. *Psychology Today*. Retrieved from

https://www.psychologytoday.com/us/blog/brain-wise/201904/the-science-habits

[2] Jakob Tanner. (2016, September 26) The science of Procrastination. *LONDNR Magazine*. Retrieved from

https://londnr.com/the-science-of-procrastination/

[3] Irving Wallace. (1977) Self control techniques of famous novelists. *Journal of Applied Behaviour analysis*. Retrieved from

https://www.ncbi.nlm.nih.gov/pmc/articles/PMC1311220/pdf/jaba00114-0143.pdf

[4] Marianna Hunt. (2018, December 30) Party tricks and naked writing: the eccentric life of Victor Hugo. *The Guardian*. Retrieved from

https://www.theguardian.com/books/booksblog/2018/dec/30/party-tricks-and-naked-writing-the-eccentric-life-of-victor-hugo

[5] Tafel, E. (1979) *Apprentice to genius: years with Frank Floyd Wright*. McGraw Hill Book Company. Retrieved from

https://archive.org/details/apprenticetogeni0000tafe

[6] Kate Connolly. (2009, November 22) Friedrich von Schiller: the Romantic lover. *The Guardian*. Retrieved from

https://www.theguardian.com/stage/2009/nov/22/friedrich-schiller-anniversary-film-biography

[7] Johnson, CB. (2013, June 4) *Odd type writers*. (1st Edition) TarcherPerigee. Retrieved from

https://www.amazon.com/exec/obidos/ASIN/0399159940/

[8] Schlicke, Paul. *Conversations with Dickens: A Fictional Dialogue Based on Biographical Facts.* Duncan Baird Publishers, 2019. Retrieved December 2, 2020.

[9] Carl Hartman. (2003, July 6) British Were Reportedly Warned of Washington's Plans. *Los Angeles Times.* Retrieved from

https://www.latimes.com/archives/la-xpm-2003-jul-06-adna-geo6-story.html

[10] Bramly, Serge. *Leonardo: Discovering the Life of Leonardo Da Vinci.* Translated by Sian Reynolds, First Edition, Harpercollins, 1991. Retrieved December 2, 2020.

[11] Issacson, Walter. *Leonardo da Vinci.* First Edition, Simon & Schuster, 2017. Retrieved December 2, 2020

[12] Paul Harris. (2005, November 20) You go, girl. *The Guardian.* Retrieved   from https://www.theguardian.com/media/2005/nov/20/television.usa

[13] Kathleen Elkins. (2015, May 28) From poverty to a $3 billion fortune — the incredible rags-to-riches story of Oprah Winfrey. *Business Insider.* Retrieved from

https://www.businessinsider.com/rags-to-riches-story-of-oprah-winfrey-2015-5

[14] Mark Frauenfelder. (2006, February 27) Benjamin Franklin's 13-point plan for virtuous living. *Boingboing.* Retrieved from

https://boingboing.net/2006/02/27/benjamin-franklins-1.html

[15] Chapman University. (2018, October 16) Chapman University Survey of American Fears. *Chapman University.* Retrieved from

https://blogs.chapman.edu/wilkinson/2018/10/16/americas-top-fears-2018/

[16] NAP. (2000) *How People Learn.* The National Academis Press. Retrieved from

https://www.nap.edu/read/9853/chapter/8#115

[17] Dr. Daniel G. Amen, MD & Dr. Mehmet Oz, MD. (n.d.) What impact does constant learning have on the brain? *Sharecare.* Retrieved from

https://www.sharecare.com/health/brain/learnings-impact-on-the-brain

[18] Harvard Medical School. (n.d.) Strengthen relationships for longer, healthier life. *Harvard Health Publishing.* Retrieved from

https://www.health.harvard.edu/healthbeat/strengthen-relationships-for-longer-healthier-life

[19] Science Daily. (2017, April 24) How walking benefits the brain. *Science Daily.* Retrieved from

https://www.sciencedaily.com/releases/2017/04/170424141340.htm

[20] Zaria Gorvett. (2017, June 12) More than 10 hours of sleep and no socks – could this be the secret to thinking like a genius? *BBC Future.* Retrieved from

https://www.bbc.com/future/article/20170612-what-you-can-learn-from-einsteins-quirky-habits

[21] Damon Young Ph.D. (2015, January 12) Charles Darwin's Daily Walks. *Psychology Today.* Retrieved from

https://www.psychologytoday.com/us/blog/how-think-about-exercise/201501/charles-darwins-daily-walks

[22] Currey, Mason. *Daily Rituals: How Artists Work.* Illustrated Edition, Knopf, 2013. Retrieved December 2, 2020

[23] Kevin Loria. (2018, April 22) Being outside can improve memory, fight depression, and lower blood pressure — here are 12 science-backed reasons to spend more time outdoors. *Business Insider.* Retrieved from

https://www.businessinsider.com/why-spending-more-time-outside-is-healthy-2017-7

[24] Pretor-Pinney, Gavin. *A Cloud a Day.* Batsford Ltd, 2019. Retrieved December 2, 2020

[25] Paul Keegan. (n.d.) Here's What Really Happened at That Company That Set a $70,000 Minimum Wage. *Inc.* Retrieved from

https://www.inc.com/magazine/201511/paul-keegan/does-more-pay-mean-more-growth.html

[26] Darwin, Charles. *The Descent of Man, and Selection in Relation to Sex.* John Murray, 1871, United Kingdom. Retrieved December 2, 2020.

[27] NZ dolphin rescues beached whales. (2008, March 12) *BBC News.* Retrieved from http://news.bbc.co.uk/2/hi/asia-pacific/7291501.stm

[28] Huff Post (2013, December 4) Leopard Cub Adopts Her Prey's Baby, Shows What We Can Learn From The Animal World. *Huff Post.* Retrieved from

https://www.huffpost.com/entry/leopard-adopts-baby-baboo_n_4386147

[29] Jenny Santi. (2015, December 1) The Science Behind the Power of Giving (Op-ed). *Live Science.* Retrieved from

https://www.livescience.com/52936-need-to-give-boosted-by-brain-science-and-evolution.html

[30] Santi, Jenny. *The Giving Way to Happiness: Stories and Science Behind the Life-Changing Power of Giving.* Penguin, 2015. Retrieved December 2, 2020

[31] David Grossman. (2014, January 24) Secret Google lab 'rewards staff for failure'. *BBC.* Retrieved from

https://www.bbc.com/news/technology-25880738

[32] Tesla, Nikola. *My Inventions and Other Writings.* Dover Publications, Inc., 2016. Retrieved December 2, 2020

[33] Kevin Kruse. (2015, July 10) Millionaires Don't use To-Do Lists. *Forbes.* Retrieved from

https://www.forbes.com/sites/kevinkruse/2015/07/10/to-do-lists-time-management/

[34] Kevin Kruse. (2016, January 20) 15 Surprising Things Productive People Do Differently. *Forbes*. Retrieved from

https://www.forbes.com/sites/kevinkruse/2016/01/20/15-surprising-things-productive-people-do-differently/#78dd7f244b27

[35] Ferriss, Timothy. *The 4-Hour Workweek: Escape 9-5, Live Anywhere, and Join the New Rich*. Harmony Books, 2012. Retrieved December 2, 2020.

[36] Deloitte. (n.d.) Questioning the 80/20 rule for health care. *Deloitte*. Retrieved from

https://www2.deloitte.com/us/en/pages/life-sciences-and-health-care/articles/is-80-20-rule-of-health-care-still-true-population-value-based.html

[37] Steven Poole. (2013, January 17) Programmer Bob who outsourced his job was a model modern employee. *The Guardian*. Retrieved from

https://www.theguardian.com/commentisfree/2013/jan/17/sacked-model-modern-employee-outsourcing

[38] Tim Ferris. (2009, July 12) How to Simplify Your Love Life. *Tim Ferris*. Retrieved from

http://blog.timferriss.com/random-thoughts-and-findings/how-to-tim-ferriss-your-love-life

[39] Nicola Twilley, Cynthia Graber & Gastropod. (2018, August 28) The 'Poison Squad' That Shook America's Faith in Preservatives. *The Atlantic*. Retrieved from

https://www.theatlantic.com/science/archive/2018/08/the-poison-squad-that-shook-americas-faith-in-preservatives/568753/

[40] Bruce Watson. (2013, June 27) The Poison Squad: An Incredible History. *Esquire*. Retrieved from

https://www.esquire.com/food-drink/food/a23169/poison-squad/

[41] Natalie Zarrelli. (2016, August 30) Food Testing in 1902 Featured a Bow Tie-Clad 'Poison Squad' Eating Plates of Acid. *Atlas Obscura*. Retrieved from

https://www.atlasobscura.com/articles/food-testing-in-1902-featured-a-tuxedoclad-poison-squad-eating-plates-of-acid

[42] Susan Weinschenk Ph.D. (2013, October 15) The Power of the Word "Because" to Get People to Do Stuff. *Psychology Today.* Retrieved from

https://www.psychologytoday.com/us/blog/brain-wise/201310/the-power-the-word-because-get-people-do-stuff

[43] Garcia, H & Miralles, F. *Ikigai: The Japanese Secret to a Long and Happy Life.* Illustarted Edition, Penguin Life, 2017. Retrieved December 2, 2020.

[44] Dan Beuttner. (n.d.) How to live to be 100+. *Ted.* Retrieved from

https://www.ted.com/talks/dan_buettner_how_to_live_to_be_10 0/transcript?language=en

[45] Jamie Ducharme. (2018, February 15) 5 Place Where People Live the Longest and Healthiest Lives. *Time.* Retrieved from

https://time.com/5160475/blue-zones-healthy-long-lives/

[46] Evernote Team. (2017, January 11) Albert Einstein's Unique Approach to Thinking. *Evernote.* Retrieved from

https://evernote.com/blog/einsteins-unique-approach-to-thinking/

[47] Ester Bloom. (2017, May 15) The self-made man is a myth, Arnold Schwarzenegger tells students. *CNBC.* Retrieved from

https://www.cnbc.com/2017/05/15/arnold-schwarzenegger-channels-elizabeth-warren-in-u-of-houston-speech.html

[48] Benefits of a Shorter Work Week. (2018, March 21) *Ohio University.* Retrieved from onlinemasters.ohio.edu/blog/benefits-of-a-shorter-work-week/.

[49] Collewet, Marion & Sauermann, Jan. "Working hours and productivity." Labour Economics, 2017. 47. 96-106. 10.1016/j.labeco.2017.03.006. Retrieved December 2, 2020

[50] Wong, Kapo, Chan, Alan H. S. and Ngan, S. C. "The Effect of Long Working Hours and Overtime on Occupational Health: A Meta-Analysis of Evidence from 1998 to 2018." *International Journal of Environmental Research and Public Health*, vol. 16, no. 12, 2019, p. 2102. doi:10.3390/ijerph16122102.

[51] Chie Matsumoto. (2019, June 14) Japan wakes up to the benefits of napping on the job. *Nikkei Asia*. Retrieved from

https://asia.nikkei.com/Life-Arts/Life/Japan-wakes-up-to-the-benefits-of-napping-on-the-job

[52] Nick Meyer. (n.d.) The NASA Studies on Napping. *Priceonomics.* Retrieved from

https://priceonomics.com/the-nasa-studies-on-napping/

[53] Adrienne Santos-Longhurst. (2019, March 19) Everything You Need to Know About the Benefits of Napping. *Healthline.* Retrieved from

https://www.healthline.com/health/how-long-should-i-nap#nap-vs-sleep

[54] Alexa Fry. (2020, October 9) Napping. *Sleep Foundation.* Retrieved from

https://www.sleepfoundation.org/articles/napping

[55] Emily Cronkleton. (2018, September 11) Wim Hof: The Man and the Method. *Healthline.* Retrieved from

https://www.healthline.com/health/wim-hof-method#research

[56] Wim Hof Method. (n.d.) The Science Behind the Wim Hof Method. *Wim Hof Method.* Retrieved from

https://www.wimhofmethod.com/science

[57] Braucher, Jean, Orbach, Barak. "Scamming: The Misunderstood Confidence Man". *Yale Journal of Law & Humanities*, Oct. 2015, pp 249–292. doi:10.2139/ssrn.2314071. S2CID 148270133.

[58] Jim Hammerand. (2012, December 11). Q&A: 'Catch Me if You Can' Conman Abagnale Tells How to Prevent Fraud. *Minneapolis Business Journal.* Retrieved from

https://www.bizjournals.com/twincities/blog/banking/2012/12/crime
-doesnt-pay-warns-catch-me-if.html?page=all

[59] Padgett, Simon. *Profiling the fraudster: removing the mask to prevent and detect fraud.* First Edition, John Wiley & Sons, p. 159. Retrieved December 2, 2020.

[60] Olivia Solon. (2017, February 12) Frank Abagnale on the death of the con artist and the rise of cybercrime. *Wired.* Retrieved from

https://www.wired.co.uk/article/frank-abagnale

[61] Susannah Bryan. (2016, October 26) Former fraudster who inspired 'Catch Me If You Can' now works to thwart scammers. Sun Sentinel. Retrieved from

https://www.sun-sentinel.com/local/broward/fl-catch-me-if-you-can-sunrise-20161026-story.html

[62] Bell, Rachael. Skywayman: The Story of Frank W. Abagnale Jr. Crime Library: Criminal Minds and Methods. Turner Entertainment Networks. p. 6, "Practicing and Evading the Law". Archived from the original on October 9, 2014. Retrieved December 2, 2020.

[63] Fortune Editors. (2011, May 10) How they failed to catch Madoff. *Fortune.* Retrieved from

https://fortune.com/2011/05/10/how-they-failed-to-catch-madoff/

[64] World Bank. (2018, October 17) *Nearly Half the World Lives on Less than $5.50 a Day.* Washington: World Bank. Retrieved from

https://www.worldbank.org/en/news/press-release/2018/10/17/nearly-half-the-world-lives-on-less-than-550-a-day

[65] Nicole Spector. (2017, November 28) Smiling can trick your brain into happiness — and boost your health. *NBC News.* Retrieved from

https://www.nbcnews.com/better/health/smiling-can-trick-your-brain-happiness-boost-your-health-ncna822591

[66] University of Tennessee at Knoxville. (2019, April 12) Psychologists find smiling really can make people happier. *Science Daily*. Retrieved from

https://www.sciencedaily.com/releases/2019/04/190412094728.htm

[67] Duhigg, Charles. The Power of Habit: Why We Do What We Do in Life and Business. Random House Trade Paperbacks, 2014. Retrieved December 2, 2020.

[68] Heath, Chip, and Heath, Dan. Switch: How to Change Things When Change Is Hard. First Edition, Crown Business, 2010. Retrieved December 2, 2020

[69] Aine Cain. (2018, September 1) 21 billionaires who grew up poor. *Business Insider*. Retrieved from

https://www.businessinsider.com/billionaires-who-came-from-nothing-2013-12#born-into-poverty-oprah-winfrey-became-the-first-african-american-tv-correspondent-in-nashville-6

[70] Jeré Longman. (2008, December 9) A 73-Year-Old Gives Basketball a Second Shot. New York Times. Retrieved from https://www.nytimes.com/2008/12/10/sports/ncaabasketball/10player.html

[71] Vanity Fair. (2012, September 5) Barack Obama to Michael Lewis on a Presidential Loss of Freedom: "You Don't Get Used to It—At Least, I Don't". Vanity Fair. Retrieved from

https://www.vanityfair.com/news/2012/09/barack-obama-michael-lewis

[72] Brenda Barbosa. (2017, June 9) Billionaire Richard Branson Does This At Every Meeting. Here's Why You Should Do It Too. Inc. Retrieved from https://www.inc.com/brenda-barbosa/the-habit-billionaire-richard-branson-swears-by-and-how-you-can-cultivate-it-to.html

[73] Andrew R. Chow. (2021, October 1) How Seinfeld Became One of TV's Great Moneymakers. Time. Retrieved from

https://time.com/6103335/seinfeld-netflix-business/

[74] Gina Trapani. (2007, July 24) Jerry Seinfeld's Productivity Secret. Lifehacker. Retrieved from

https://lifehacker.com/jerry-seinfelds-productivity-secret-281626

[75] Ali Binazir. (2011, June 15) What Are Chances You Would Be Born. Harvard. Retrieved from

http://blogs.harvard.edu/abinazir/2011/06/15/what-are-chances-you-would-be-born/

[76] GQ Sports. (2020, July 23) How Kobe Bryant's Trainer Helped Him Become a Legend. GQ Sports. Retrieved from

https://youtu.be/YG6ZU-Azttc

[77] Alon, I. (2003). *Chinese culture, Organizational Behavior, and International Business Management*. Praeger.

www.ingramcontent.com/pod-product-compliance
Lightning Source LLC
Chambersburg PA
CBHW071317130726
47996CB00002B/517